T0323992

Cambridge Elements ☰

Elements in Twenty-First Century Music Practice
edited by
Simon Zagorski-Thomas
London College of Music, University of West London

CROSS-CULTURAL COLLABORATION IN POPULAR MUSIC

Practice-Based Research

Toby Martin
University of Sydney

Seyed MohammadReza Beladi
University of Huddersfield

Đăng Lan
Independent Scholar

CAMBRIDGE
UNIVERSITY PRESS

Shaftesbury Road, Cambridge CB2 8EA, United Kingdom

One Liberty Plaza, 20th Floor, New York, NY 10006, USA

477 Williamstown Road, Port Melbourne, VIC 3207, Australia

314–321, 3rd Floor, Plot 3, Splendor Forum, Jasola District Centre,
New Delhi – 110025, India

103 Penang Road, #05–06/07, Visioncrest Commercial, Singapore 238467

Cambridge University Press is part of Cambridge University Press & Assessment,
a department of the University of Cambridge.

We share the University's mission to contribute to society through the pursuit of
education, learning and research at the highest international levels of excellence.

www.cambridge.org
Information on this title: www.cambridge.org/9781009454117

DOI: 10.1017/9781009358255

First published 2024

A catalogue record for this publication is available from the British Library

ISBN 978-1-009-45411-7 Hardback
ISBN 978-1-009-35824-8 Paperback
ISSN 2633-4585 (online)
ISSN 2633-4577 (print)

Cambridge University Press & Assessment has no responsibility for the persistence
or accuracy of URLs for external or third-party internet websites referred to in this
publication and does not guarantee that any content on such websites is, or will
remain, accurate or appropriate.

Cross-Cultural Collaboration in Popular Music

Practice-Based Research

Elements in Twenty-First Century Music Practice

DOI: 10.1017/9781009358255
First published online: December 2024

Toby Martin
University of Sydney

Seyed MohammadReza Beladi
University of Huddersfield

Đăng Lan
Independent Scholar

Author for correspondence: Toby Martin, toby.martin@sydney.edu.au

Abstract: Cross-cultural collaboration in popular music represents opportunities for the audibility of multiple voices and the creation of new sounds, but it also presents many challenges. These challenges are both musical – that is, how to technically match voices – and ethical – that is, how to negotiate historically entrenched power discrepancies. Practice-based research has recently developed as a field in popular music studies. This burgeoning area has much to offer in terms of new knowledge, based on embodied insights, lived experience, and an arts practice. Through a practitioner-centred account of three projects involving traditional Persian and Vietnamese musicians, and western folk/rock musicians, this Element suggests pragmatic strategies and conceptual frameworks for making pop music with people of different cultural backgrounds.

Keywords: practice-led research, cross-cultural collaboration, songwriting, composition, popular music studies

ISBNs: 9781009454117 (HB), 9781009358248 (PB), 9781009358255 (OC)
ISSNs: 2633-4585 (online), 2633-4577 (print)

Contents

Because the music is very immense, no limit. So the more you go through music and the more you find out – something else, something else, something else – the more you want to know.

– Đăng Lan

1 Prologue

MohammadReza

It was the year 2017 and, as always, I was doing my daily chores in the small shop that my wife and I ran. I had been out of Iran for a few years, and I was living in England with my wife and son. I had a dance and music group, and such activities were not easy in Iran, especially after the revolution.[1] For a long time, I only did my artistic activities abroad, even when I was living in Iran. Since coming to England, I had tried to continue my artistic work somehow. Russia, Qatar, Oman, Spain, and France were the places where I performed in the years after I left Iran. My group was still in Iran, and I managed things from England.

To be able to stand on our own two feet, we decided to open a small business, a sandwich shop, at Queensgate Market near the University of Huddersfield. That day, as on other days, some customers were queuing up when I noticed that there was a person among them who seemed to want to say something. I thought he was a customer who had something else to say. He waited until it was quiet and then told me that he had been told I was a musician.

I had photos of my group displayed in the shop, so it wasn't hard to guess that I was in the music business. In fact, sometimes the customers started talking about that and I felt good telling them about my artistic activities. This time it was different. Meeting this person, who I later found out was Toby Martin, a university lecturer, was the beginning of new extensive artistic and research activities for me that continue to this day.

I remember we had a good conversation and it felt good to talk about music with another professional like Toby. At that time Toby had a music project in hand where he was writing music based on the stories of immigrants or refugees and he asked me to be part of it. A few times he and I went to a church where refugees from different countries had gathered. It was an interesting atmosphere, with people from different cultural backgrounds; some could play instruments, and a few were singers.

Toby also asked me to attend one of his classes as a guest lecturer at the university and talk about the music of Bushehr. It didn't take long until I was able to apply for a master's course. That same year, 2018, we had a joint

---

[1] The Iranian Islamic Revolution 1979.

performance at the local Democracy Week 'Making Music Democratically', while I accompanied Toby's guitar with my dammam.[2] A few years have since passed and my artistic collaboration with Toby, and more importantly our friendship, continues.

Đăng Lan

In Saigon, I performed on television, in clubs, and on radio. I performed mostly in 'Tea Clubs'. These were like dance clubs, but the audience had to remain seated. Madame Nhu, the wife of the vice-president of South Vietnam, did not allow people to dance. At that time you could not dance in the club, you could only listen. Because there was no dancing, it was like a tea room. It was like chamber music. A chamber music club.

The club I performed in mostly was called the Queen Bee club. I sang almost every night at the Queen Bee from 1971–1973. I sang with a club band, in a Western style. With this band I did Western classical songs like 'Blue Danube'. This was mostly for Vietnamese audiences, but there were also all kinds of Asian audiences, and sometimes I had to sing in Chinese and Japanese for the customers. But there were no American soldiers – they didn't go to those kinds of clubs, they went to bars. The band also played rock music, pop music, Western style, and did all types of songs; some singers did the twist for instance (but no dancing!). The Queen Bee also had a special traditional band that would play for about fifteen minutes every night, before the Western-style music began. I sang traditional Vietnamese songs with this band.

Now with the new band, in Australia, with Toby and Bree and Mohammed, I never thought I could play such music. I never believed it. I never thought I could play Western style on Vietnamese instruments. But working with these musicians meant I could find out who I am and what I could do.

When I first played with the band, it felt very interesting. I have to say that I had never played with such a band before. The first time I played with them I felt like we had been playing together for a long time. Maybe we played together in a previous life, I don't know. This was the first time I played Western style but on traditional Vietnamese instruments. I felt so excited, I felt like a new person. When I play with this band, I can wear jeans, I can wear Western style. I like it. My friends would ask me 'why do you like to play with an Australian band?' and I would say 'because I feel free'. I feel very natural. I can wear anything I like.

---

[2] www.hud.ac.uk/news/2018/october/local-democracy-making-music-democratically/, accessed 3 August 2023.

Toby Martin

I pull up outside a suburban house in south-west Sydney. I get my guitar out of the car and walk down the side path and into the backyard. Five cats run under the house. The backyard is full of abundant fruit trees – mango, longan, guava – and polystyrene boxes overflowing with herbs. Trestle tables are covered in drying fruit. It is midsummer and the air is humid and heavy. Banana trees are starting to sway in the growing wind. There are three pairs of slip-on shoes at the back door.

I put my guitar down on its end, lean on it, and shout out 'Hi, I am here!' Inside, a television is playing CNN's ongoing report of the attempted White House coup. Lan is standing in the kitchen. There are piles of Vietnamese-language newspapers on the floral tablecloth, and a stack of cassettes by the computer. A đàn bầu is hard up against the wall by the dining table. It is plugged into a battery-powered amp.

Lan and I hug. There hasn't been a lot of hugging during Covid-19 and this still feels strange. She tells me to sit down and brings over a plate. She says 'in Vietnam, you always eat before starting something'. It is a plate of what she calls 'international spaghetti', pasta with tomato, fresh herbs, and kim chi. Lan is laughing; she thinks it is hilarious, this combination of flavours. I start laughing too. 'No-one else makes this. You won't find this anywhere else! It is like the music we make,' Lan says.

After eating, the plates are cleared away and the table turns into a small rehearsal studio. Lan pulls out a microphone and sings along to a pre-recorded backing track. It is a contemporary pop arrangement of a well-known Vietnamese anti-war folk song. There is a long section of dramatic spoken word – a recitation. The CNN channel is still blaring in the background.

Then we pull out sheaves of lyrics, hand-written in Vietnamese and printed in English. The lyrics are a Vietnamese version of a Lord Byron poem, re-translated back into English. The rain is falling now, overflowing from the gutters, beading the windows. I pull out my acoustic guitar and we bend down, concentrating on the lyrics, as we sing. We take it in turns to sing our verses; but when we come together for the finale, we lock eyes for a dramatic final note. Then we fall apart into laughing . . . 'yeah yeah, that's it!'

We then move onto a long story song; Lan sings in English about Buddhism and the birth of her son. My guitar is de-tuned and droning. It's far from perfect; there are many starts and stops. Next, Lan switches on her amp and begins to pluck the đàn bầu. I stamp my foot in time and try to find the right accompany-ing part on guitar. The song is a well-known Vietnamese song, but the way we play it draws on indie-folk and rock.

The jam session ends and we walk outside into the post-rain freshness.

2 Introduction

Faced with this Element on cross-cultural collaboration in popular music, you would be well entitled to ask, 'What popular music *isn't* cross-cultural?' After all, a sense of cultures and sounds merging is at the heart of so many musical genres of the twentieth and twenty-first centuries. Country music is a blending of British Isles folk music and African American forms (with Latin and Eastern European influences thrown into the mix); rock 'n' roll is a combination of country and blues; electronic dance music is the result of cross-pollination between black American disco cultures and German minimal electronica; while hip-hop is a mash-up of Latin and Black street cultures, which merged with hard rock elements in the 1980s. Not to mention that the traditional folk music of Bushehr in southern Iran is made up of music from many different cultures of the region, and that Vietnamese popular music has since the late colonial period been strongly influenced by Western music (Norton 2009; Beladi 2021). While popular music genres swiftly cohere and have the sense of having always been there, they invariably have a core of collage and experimentation.

Popular music history is rife with examples of power imbalances and the exploitation of artists of colour and minorities. The rise in popularity of so-called 'world music' in the late twentieth century, known by other names earlier in the century, was accompanied by critiques that pointed out its exploitation and othering of non-Western artists for the sake of improving the sales of global record labels and reviving the flagging careers of pop stars (Erlmann 1999; Bohlman 2002; Turino 2003; Rodano and Olanyian 2016). However, merging musical genres can also create the possibility to hear multiple, diverse voices and a sense of understanding and connectivity across cultures and, if ethically handled, the possibility of equally shared career and financial advancement.

Popular music is often based on dialogue between musical cultures and, sometimes, between people from different cultures. This Element is not the history of these musical and social relationships, but it offers some snapshot examples of these processes at work. Popular music history is also replete with examples of music that is accidentally, circumstantially, or commercially cross-cultural. What we offer here is slightly different – projects that were deliberately cross-cultural for artistic and research purposes. The three projects we examine here were conceived as a way to make interesting pop music, but also to test what was possible when people from very different backgrounds sit down to make music together. What happens when, for example, post-punk–style, alternative-tuned guitars are merged with Arabic and Persian modal forms; a Vietnamese folk song is re-arranged as an indie rock song; or two people with vast differences in their lived experiences and cultural backgrounds write lyrics together about living in the same city? Behind these projects was a spirit of inquiry and experimentation, an intention to test the limits of collaboration, as well as a concern to make music that works as 'pop' music and could find an audience (ideally a large one!).

The music we are discussing in the case studies in this Element is quite specific in instrumentation and in recording methodology. It is predominantly acoustic, using drum kits, amped guitars, and stringed instruments. It uses traditional forms of verse/chorus songwriting. It does not have many of the production features of early twenty-first-century music such as programmed drums, 808 synths, click tracks, and trap hi-hats. Which is not to make any value judgements about any approach to music making, but is to say that while we are framing our work as 'popular music' we are using that definition more as an approach to creation than as a style, or a sign of popularity. As Shuker (2016: 2–5) outlines, it can be problematic to define popular music using aesthetic criteria alone (as the term can encompass everything from the most rustic of folk, to the most glittering of dance pop), or using socio-economic criteria (as what to do with steadfastedly underground genres such as black metal?). Rather, it may make more sense to regard many types of music as being made within a field of 'popular music culture', a term which might refer to 'the ways of making' and the 'practices associated with these processes' (2).

Some commentators prefer the term 'contemporary' music in order to differentiate styles, such as hip-hop, country, and r 'n' b, from popular music of the past, such as classical music, traditional musics, and big band swing music. However, we feel that contemporary music is too broad a term for our uses, as it can also include 'experimental', or 'new' music, which draws on traditions, literature, and frameworks different to the ones we are using. All in all, it might make sense to say we are viewing our own contributions to contemporary music through a popular music studies lens.

This Element is an examination of music from the inside, from those who are playing it and composing it. In this respect, it joins with other scholars in arts research and ethnomusicology exploring embodied research practices. This Element is practitioner-centred and its methodology is practice-based research. We offer here accounts of music making that are based in embodied lived experience, through our practice as musicians. Throughout the Element we reflect on the ways in which research of this kind might produce new or different insights to those created by observer-based research or text-based research, although we also highly value these other approaches and draw on them as well.[3]

---

[3] A note on terminology. We have used the term 'practice-based' but acknowledge that there are many other useful terms that other scholars prefer, such as 'practice-led', 'practice research', 'arts research', and 'research-creation'. We find that the term '-based' best encapsulates the idea of

This Element has two research questions that underpin it, one pragmatic, the other political. Firstly, how can musicians from different cultural backgrounds make music together that works musically, and particularly that works as pop music? As Zagorski-Thomas (2014: 46) wrote, in a provocation that is relevant to our project, how can theory inform the practicalities of music making? Secondly, how can musicians from different cultural backgrounds mindfully and ethically negotiate the power imbalances inherent to these projects? These questions are addressed by interrogating our interpersonal relationships as much as our musical relationships. The questions ask us to reconsider our roles as people, as much as our roles as musicians. Or, to flip it, being mindful musicians might offer us a model for how to be ethical people, to enact a form of 'artistic citizenship' (Elliott et al. 2016; Carfoot 2016). In addition to our practitioner-based research inquiries, this Element will also develop a theoretical framework based around literature on practice-based research, intercultural arts research, examples of co-produced research, and post-colonial work in ethnomusicology and critical ethnography.

In keeping with the research questions, we hope that our contribution to new knowledge will be both practical and conceptual. Through our own work, we will outline musical strategies that have been useful and that other musicians might employ when embarking on projects like these, as well as interpersonal strategies that might help navigate the complex terrain of working in this way. We will also suggest ways in which theories of co-production can be applied to a popular music-making context.

This Element will focus on three projects, all of which the authors have been involved with as songwriters, composers, and musicians. The first is *Songs from Northam Avenue*, an evocation of western Sydney via narrative-based songwriting and collaboration among Arabic, Vietnamese, and Western musicians. The second, *Song Khúc Lượn Bay/ Two Sounds Gliding*, is a collaboration between two songwriters with very different backgrounds, Lan and Toby, and is an attempt to find a meeting place between Vietnamese traditional music and Western folk/rock. The third is *I Felt the Valley Lifting*, an album of songs about modern village life in northern, post-industrial England, and a collaboration between Persian and British Isles folk and rock musicians.

---

practice being at the core of what we do as researchers, but can be extrapolated out and built on from there. We also use the term 'cross-cultural' rather than 'intercultural'. We find that the hyphen and the idea of a cross movement of ideas rather than an integrated one better encapsulates the idea of cultures talking to each other, but remaining distinct rather than necessarily merging and combining (although that might happen too).

All three projects had different methods of collaboration which were dependent on particular circumstances including who initiated the project, the musicians involved, how the projects were financed, and the time available. They also had their own specific goals and outcomes. They were different from each other, and indeed we maintain that a key part of cross-cultural collaboration is being flexible, able to react to different collaborative environments, and being able to work with what is in front of you and around you. Nevertheless, we also think that the variety of musicians involved here; the length of time these projects took, stretching over several years for each one; and the comparison of approaches means that our findings have broader applicability and will be of interest to others practicing or researching in the field.

Our intention with the writing style of this Element is to reflect the content in its form. One of our hopes with cross-cultural collaboration is to create music where different voices are heard, sometimes distinctly, sometimes melded. We also tried to do this in the writing. We all have different ways of communicating our ideas. At the time of writing, Toby Martin has been a full-time, continuing academic for nine years, and MohammadReza has just finished his PhD and works as a sessional academic, and both have several academic publications (in both English and Persian) to their names. Lan does not work as an academic and her tone is more conversational, often with a poetic charge to it that traditional scholarly writing can obscure. We thought it important to preserve the original tone. Parts written by the individual authors – mostly in Sections 5–9 – are indicated as such at the beginning of each sub-section, and by indentation. As Toby prompted the other authors to write these sections, his parts often provide linkage and context between practice-led testimony. Other parts – mostly in Sections 1–4 and the conclusion – have been written up by Toby but draw on ideas and frameworks from all three authors. In writing this Element, Lan and Toby recorded themselves talking and recalling aspects of the project and in this were following on from Östersjö et al. 2023 and their methodology of stimulated recall. Some of this conversation is presented here verbatim in order to capture the different viewpoints and the to-and-fro dialogue that characterised the projects.

All three albums discussed here are available via major streaming services, and we have provided YouTube links for them. Rather than providing individual hyperlinks for each song, we thought it would be better for readers to be able to listen to each individual song when relevant, or spend some time listening as an activity separate from reading the Element.

The links are:

Songs from Northam Avenue: www.youtube.com/watch?v=h_XIoV38Lb
   A&list=OLAK5uy_kjgWBYwqkVhRU9N97qr3XUwqyphVsUnps
Khúc Lượn Bay/Two Sounds Gliding: www.youtube.com/watch?v=Nqfefe
   bZMD8&list=OLAK5uy_l5o1X9VUGrIqFknzrd6N3Ux8souvc8dzQ
   www.youtube.com/watch?v=NqfefebZMD8&list=OLAK5uy_l5o1X9VUGr
   IqFknzrd6N3Ux8souvc8dzQ
I Felt the Valley Lifting: www.youtube.com/watch?v=hTH2Cfzp
   IXw&list=OLAK5uy_mjd_Ge_b7f9SwwljMAwMD6Yc0I5w-WT1w www.you
   tube.com/watch?v=hTH2CfzpIXw&list=OLAK5uy_mjd_Ge_b7f9SwwljM
   AwMD6Yc0I5w-WT1w

Before we look at the detail of our projects and their findings, we will outline some of the previous scholarly work on practice-based research, particularly as it pertains to popular music, to cross-cultural collaboration, to work in adjacent fields such as ethnomusicology, and to co-produced research in other disciplines. This section is not meant as a comprehensive literature review, but rather as an overview of the concepts that we found helpful in developing our own methodological framework. These sections will be followed by a short overview of each of our musical and cultural backgrounds, a section on each project, and the strategies employed, before discussing our general findings in the conclusion.

3 Practice-Based Research Methodologies

As scholars and practitioners have argued, an arts practice can be a form of research and create new knowledge. This has aligned with a recent trend in the humanities to value insight that is based on lived experience of something from the inside, which asks different questions and provides different answers to a study of something from the outside. To some extent, this turn has been driven by the fact that arts practitioners increasingly find themselves employed by research institutions and are competing for research funding. As such, they *need* to frame what they do as research. But, interestingly, this re-framing can have profound consequences for the type of work they do. Forced to ask new questions of their practice, practitioner-researchers often do things they had not thought of doing before, and create new types of music.

Anthropologist Tim Ingold has proposed the importance of 'knowing from the inside' and 'thinking through making' (Ingold 2013: 7). Within the world of arts research, Robin Nelson has argued for the way that creative practice is 'knowledge-producing in its own right', which we have found a useful and resonant aphorism (Nelson 2013: 48). Nelson writes that practice-based research is usefully thought of in two parts: inquiry through practice, and 'the practice' as evidence/output of the research (8; see also McLaughlin 2015). Nelson also discusses the importance of writing about research, saying that much arts knowledge is implicit, embodied, unconscious, and unexpressed. This is, of course, part of its value. Yet reflection on a practice 'allows for the making visible of an intelligence which nevertheless remains fundamentally located in embodied knowing' (41). Following on from that, we regard the 'inquiry' part to be the music making itself, the 'evidence' part to be the recorded albums and concerts, and the 'translation' of the evidence to be this Element.

In *The Minor Gesture* philosopher and practising artist Erin Manning argues that 'research-creation' – her phrase – is not just 'knowledge-producing in its own right', but also might produce knowledge and insights that are different to those produced by other types of research. Manning asks, 'How does a practice that involves making open the way for a different idea of what can be termed knowledge?' Manning is proposing a scenario where the art process itself is 'generative of thought', rather than the research component being generated by the writing about the art (Manning 2016: 11 and 240), an important distinction. The title of Manning's book, *The Minor Gesture*, suggests the myriad ways in which activities and inquiries that lie beyond, or underneath, traditional research – and indeed traditional and neurotypical ways of thinking – might lead to new ways of thinking and new forms of knowledge. This includes thinking about art as an artful process rather than an end result, considering neurodiverse perspectives, and considering poetic and nuanced responses to the world. We propose that songwriting and music making in cross-cultural settings might be considered a form of 'minor gesture' in that it goes subtly against the grain of ways of making music that rely on notation, and text or interview-based forms of research.

It is useful to think about practice-based research as leading to insights into two separate areas. One: insights into the way we create and perform the musical material itself. Two: insights into sociocultural issues that music making might lead to. This is an important aspect of practice-based research, as it demonstrates the way in which music is not just ornamental or aesthetically pleasing, but can lead to insights that reflect lived experience, inform attitudes to social issues, and can lead to cultural and policy changes.

As one example, the Distant Voices project in Scotland is a collaboration between popular music scholars, criminologists, musicians, and people with lived experience of the criminal justice system. These people are paired with songwriters and asked to write songs about their experiences. The results are a series of insights into the ways in which people experience incarceration and surveillance (Urie et al. 2019; Various artists 2018; Distant Voices website, www.voxliminis.co.uk/projects/distant-voices/). This is reflected in Toby's own work doing songwriting projects at HM Leeds Prison, which yielded insights into the way prisoners felt about 'home'. Songwriting showed that rather than necessarily being a place longed for, home was a source of anxiety. 'Will things be the same?/ Will they even know my name?' went the lyrics of one song. Insights that came from songwriting were unexpected, poetic, and loaded with dark irony. Songwriting carries the potential for meaning-making and in this case the prison context of the songwriting – with the particular ramifications of the idea of 'home' – provided an especially layered and charged meaning.

One of the researchers on the Distant Voices project, Jo Collinson-Scott, has written about what popular music practice can offer in terms of research insight. She asks 'how does music help us imagine differently?' Collinson-Scott makes the useful distinction between music *as* research, rather than music *alongside* research (i.e. as a fun illustration of a more weighty point) or research on the *effects* of music (i.e. the effectiveness of music in therapeutic settings). Rather, music, and particularly songwriting, can create a form of knowledge on a subject that complements other types of research (i.e. data collection, text analysis, or interviews). The resultant music 'exists as an embodied form of knowledge on the subject'. For example, in the area of supervision and surveillance, music can explore what 'supervision feels like, sounds like' (Collinson-Scott 2018). Our Element is primarily concerned with insights into how we create music, but it also has broader ramifications for social/cultural issues, such as cross-cultural connections.

On Practice-Based Research in Popular Music

Philip Tagg (2011) highlighted the way in which pop music practitioners are sometimes seen as annoying appendages to pop music studies – and argued that they should be embraced. And indeed over the last decade there has been considerable momentum in this field, with pop music practitioner-researchers exploring ways to communicate their findings. For example, the 21st Century Music Practice Research Network has a number of associated publications, both traditional and non-traditional, and focussed seminars, that seek to answer specific research questions about music composition and production through practice (for example, Exarchos 2020). In addition, a 2017 issue of *IASPM@Journal* published peer-reviewed sound recordings as research outputs accompanied by a short written exegesis (Koszolko 2017; Wolinski 2017).

In fact, to follow on from Manning's (2016) argument that an arts practice may open up different ideas of what might be termed 'knowledge', by extension a popular music practice might open up different ideas from other types of arts practices. This might be to do with specific ways of working, especially the importance of collaboration in creating popular music, but also might be to do with popular music's impulses towards the generalisable and universal. Collinson-Scott has responded to scholars that have argued that art cannot be 'knowledge' because knowledge has to be general, and art is personal/ specific, stating that 'it is my understanding that a key skill of a popular music songwriter, is to take an image or a concept and imagine exactly its generalisability' (Collinson-Scott 2018; Stévance and Lacasse 2018; Elkins 2005). In other words, popular music has a specific ability to create knowledge because of its interest in universality and generalisability.

This also is a useful counterargument to the one that contends it is problematic to consider popular music as research because of its commercial ends. Miguel Mera (2015) makes a distinction between a popular music practice that is undertaken for commercial reasons, and therefore does not align with research aims, and popular music that is 'experimental' and indeed 'unpopular' and therefore can be considered research, as long as it is not governed by the 'systems of late capitalism' (17 mins–24 mins). This type of dualism does not seem particularly useful. Just because a musical project has commercial aims does not necessarily render it un-exploratory. And further, there is a vast middle ground between music that is fringe and experimental and that which makes a lot of money (a middle ground we feel our projects occupy).

We agree with Collinson-Scott (2018) that popular music is useful precisely *because* it has universalist, or commercial, expectations. Popular music often deals in clichés; however, rather than attempting to explain this away or sweep it under the rug, we think it is better to acknowledge this and examine how pop songwriting grapples productively with the idea of cliché. Attempting to universalise a human experience is the essence of cliché, and turning a specific experience into a universal one is one of the key aspects of songwriting (indeed you might say it is a cliché of songwriting). Also, the academic impulse to develop generalised 'findings' based on 'examples' or 'evidence' follows a similar trajectory. In this, pop songwriting and academic research seem a remarkably good fit.

Practice-Based Research, Ethnomusicology, and Autoethnography

Practitioner-centred research is also a central methodology of other disciplines, especially ethnomusicology. Learning to perform a particular music genre is a 'key element of the ethnomusicological approach' (Dawe 2015: 25; see also Hitchins 2013). Mantle Hood (1982) advocated for 'bi-musicality' – which came to mean western musicians learning to perform in non-Western styles as a research method. Later, John Baily argued for the idea of ethnomusicologists 'learning to perform' and through this gaining insights into social, political, and cultural structures (Hood 1982 and Baily 2001 in McKerrell 2022). Many others have since challenged and updated these ideas, pointing out the ways in which these previous theories were Eurocentric, and that ethnomusicology could also think about how the end musical product could be 'research' (McKerrell 2022). McKerrell has also argued that ethnomusicology should begin using performance as a research outcome in itself, as a way to 'translate' cultural knowledge and as a way to prioritise performative, embodied knowledge. McKerrell (2022) urges researchers to 'embrace the performative turn and recognise the truth of embodied experience and its research potential' (21).

For Baily, Hood, and others, learning other types of music is a means to an end: a way to understand other cultures. Baily also suggested that 'musical relationships' could form the basis for 'social relationships' (Baily 2001: 96). This resonates with us, and indeed we might say that making music together is a means to various ends – to aid in cross-cultural social relationships and understanding, to help create political change, in particular to act against the vilification of migrants and migrant cultures, and to have interesting musical outcomes.

Many recent projects have focussed on the ways in which participation in music making, and music education, can lead to positive outcomes for refugees or migrants and how this affects their inclusion and integration into the host culture (Sarrouy 2023; Vougioukalou et al. 2019; Marsh 2012).[4] Rather than having integration as its frame, other projects consider how music making can affect and change the attitudes of host cultures through music. For instance, Sounding Out Refugee Stories was a project Toby was involved with, alongside two researchers from the University of Huddersfield's Business School Deema Refai and Radi Haloub. Refai – whose mother tongue is Arabic – conducted interviews with male and female refugees from Syria, currently residing in Jordan, focusing on the motivation of those who started their own businesses. The resulting interviews were translated, transcribed, turned into song lyrics and performed by local musicians and singers, leading to performances at the University of Petra and a high school in Jordan. The song project and the performances created considerable media interest in Jordan.[5] These songs showed the resourceful and entrepreneurial work done by Syrian refugees and

---

[4] https://yousound.eu/, accessed 9 September 23.
[5] www.youtube.com/watch?v=mFruTnYeJAE, accessed 15 October 23.

combatted negative images of refugees as being a drain on the system and a burden to taxpayers.[6]

In fact, as much as community music and participatory music projects are part of our frame, also relevant is what is happening in popular music where new migrants reinvigorate musical scenes, draw attention to musical cultures of their countries of origin, and show the exciting ways in which musical blending can happen. Zambia-born, Botswana-raised, Australian-based hip-hop artist Sampa the Great demonstrates strong pan-African content in her work. Her music has been immensely popular and has won numerous awards, and in doing so shows the ways in which pan-African cultures are Australian cultures, and indeed global cultures, too (Clark 2021).

McKerrell has also noted that researchers who perform music are 'subject to the same ethical problems of positionality for the researcher and the researched that emerge through fieldwork in talk and text'. While artistic researchers, or co-musicians, do things together, in an embodied way, it still stands that 'privilege, prejudice and power can be performed non-verbally' (McKerrell 2022: 14) In this, self-interrogation is an important step in 'de-colonising ethnomusicology' (Nooshin 2014: 2) in order to erode boundaries and 'to seek out commonalities and to challenge binary constructions such as East/West' (6).

Looking at the researcher's own positionality, a form of autoethnography, the researcher interrogates themselves as well as the culture they are researching, in order to gauge what types of assumptions and baggage they bring to the process: 'those with power are frequently less aware of or at least willing to acknowledge its existence as well as their role in maintaining inequitable social and cultural capital' (Hughes, Pennington, and Makris 2012: 212). Interrogating our own positionality has been an important part of our projects too, as we will discuss in the next section.

We propose that a musical practice can not only facilitate learning *about* another culture but also learning *alongside* people from other cultures, and therein learning together. Consequently, the insights that are generated from our research are not so much about another culture per se, but about the ways in which people from other cultures can work together to produce something new. This is another valuable ingredient that a pop music practice might bring to practice-based research, and as such draws on but is different to new directions in ethnomusicology.

---

[6] www.hud.ac.uk/news/2019/july/entrepreneurial-potential-of-refugees-huddersfield/, accessed 29 September 23.

We are hopeful that practice-led research will continue to emerge as a powerful new methodology in popular music studies. We are interested in how practice-based research from other disciplines can assist in this emergence. However, we are also interested in flipping this – in examining what a pop music practice can offer this broad inter-disciplinary field. Following on from Collinson-Scott, Ingold, Manning, McKerrell and others, we maintain that makers, practitioners, and musicians have much to offer not just about the way pop music works and its possibilities for innovation, but also for ideas about the ways in which knowledge is generated.

4 Cross-Cultural Music Making and Co-produced Research: Literature and Context

Cross-cultural artistic work is full of potential problems. Centuries of colonial and imperial history and the continuing disparities in wealth and privilege produced by globalisation have produced entrenched power imbalances in western society. The lack of visibility of non-Western musical forms, and the historic treatment of people of colour as 'other' means that non-Western music is often treated as exotic flavouring. bell hooks has described the ways in which Western artistic production has frequently used ethnicity as 'spice' (hooks 1992)[7]. In the Australian context, Ghassan Hage (1998) has outlined the ways in which official governmental policies of multiculturalism since the 1970s, and the resultant sociocultural milieu, has produced what he describes as 'cosmopolitan whiteness' or 'white multiculturalism'. For Hage, like hooks, this type of multiculturalism is based on the idea of consumption wherein the food, music, clothes, and rituals of non-Western migrant cultures are there to be consumed, yet this consumption is always within the framework of Western culture. In recent years, the term 'multiculturalism' has been replaced with 'diversity', but similar criticisms persist. Sara Ahmed (2012) has discussed how diversity has become a marketing term, an aesthetic way of rebranding an organisation. Diversity becomes a way of showcasing difference 'without any commitment to action or redistributive justice' and is in fact a 'containment strategy' (Ahmed 2012: 53).

In a musical context, Dylan Robinson (2020) has outlined a theory of 'fit' – where Indigenous musicians have been 'structurally accommodated' to make them 'fit' into Western art music composition and performance (5). Sometimes this can present itself as a 'fixation' on 'Indigenous content, but not Indigenous structure' (6). In this framework, Indigenous performers are offered space in a

---

[7] 'bell hooks' is spelt with lower case.

musical work, but do not control the modes of production, such as the choice of a venue or relationships with the audience (6). A key metaphor here is that of 'extractivism' – where Indigenous knowledge (not to mention resources and land) is assumed to be there for the taking, and once extracted is assimilated into white structures (14).

Taking a historical approach, Veit Erlmann (1999) has pointed out the many parallels that exist between nineteenth-century Eurocentric ideas of the panorama – of everything being able to be viewed as exotic spectacle – and postmodern, neo-liberal ideas of global consumption (181). Further, in regards to what is produced and consumed, referencing Edward Said, Erlmann states that one of the strongest hallmarks of modernity is the 'juxtaposition of the familiar and the alien, the commonplace and the exotic' (182). This connects with Torgovnik's (1990) exploration of the role 'primitivism' has played in modern art. Erlmann also points out – in specific reference to Paul Simon's *Graceland* – that the late twentieth century has seen the marketing of 'songwriter-musician as culture hero' (184), one who appears to stand their ground against prevailing trends, and stands for issues, such as the inclusion of disparate global voices (but invariably also for the songwriter-hero's own career and commercial benefit).

These were all critical – and often uncomfortable – issues for us and for our projects. Given the scale of the problems of music making in this context, it is naïve to think that our projects can avoid them. Toby, is a white, male, native-English speaking, middle-class person, with full-time employment in a university. Lan and MohammadReza are Asian, both refugees and both often working in situations where they are not speaking their first language. And Lan is a woman, and also has many caring responsibilities. While the positive and healthy exploration of these differences is precisely what this Element is about, these differences were also potentially exploitative. We were aware that in trying to make music with people of different cultures we might perpetuate power imbalances, and showcase, rather than explore, difference. Throughout this Element we have tried to be transparent in outlining not just the musical processes, but also the decision making about the shape and direction of the project. Indeed, it was partly due to discomfort around the processes and decision making of *Songs from Northam Avenue* that led us to the subsequent project *Two Sounds Gliding*. This Element is certainly not claiming to have the categorical answers to these very thorny questions, although we do hope to show that we have mindfully grappled with them. In the following sections we will outline some frameworks that helped guide our artistic processes and our thinking around these issues.

Artistic Citizenship

We have been guided by the idea of artistic citizenship (Elliott, Silverman, and Bowman 2016). That is, the idea that 'the arts can and should be "put to work" towards the positive transformation of people's lives' and that 'social/ethical responsibility lies at the heart of responsible artistic practice' (3). While our primary goal was to make interesting music for an audience rather than make 'community music' (Turino 2016: 301), there is still a strong ethical component. The music that we make has a role in voicing stories and sounds that are not heard in mainstream Anglophone society, in providing creative and employment opportunities for musicians who are marginalised, and for enabling a musical dialogue between people of different backgrounds which transforms us as individuals and provides an example of how this might be done.

There are many possible ways of being 'artistic citizens', but the ethical dimension to the projects discussed here is largely to do with the ways in which we conduct ourselves as individuals in the musical process. In this, the definition of 'praxis' by Elliott, Silverman, and Bowman (2016) is useful:

> a 'multidimensional concept that includes active reflection and critically reflective action guided by an informed ethical disposition to act rightly, with continuous concern for protecting and advancing the well-being of others . . . . Praxial art making thus consists of thoughtful and careful (i.e., "care-full") artistic practice, of artistic action that is embedded in and responsive to ever-changing social, cultural, and political circumstances.' (7)

Bartleet and Carfoot (2016) have problematised the idea of artistic citizenship, pointing out that people's citizenship status is not equal, but rather is 'differentiated' (341). This is especially the case in countries like Australia and the UK (where our projects took place) where ideas of citizenship are inextricable from violent dispossession and colonialism (341). In terms of literal citizenship, Lan and MohammadReza both arrived in new countries as refugees, and consequently their citizenship has been contingent and negotiated, whereas Toby was born into the country he is a citizen of and is a member of its dominant culture. Bartleet and Carfoot point out that in such settings, inequities are entrenched and the relinquishing of power and privilege is a huge challenge that requires constant self-evaluation (342 and 344): 'The risk is that the very politics and power dynamics we are trying to critique, we end up replicating and reinscribing' (344). Some ways to mitigate the reinforcing of power structures is to engage in long-term relationships which are *transformational* rather than *transactional*, and are characterised by 'thick reciprocity' and mutual benefits for all parties (Bartleet and Carfoot: 353, italics in original). We also acknowledge that the ability to engage in music making that seeks to create social change is itself dependent on privileges and freedoms that are often taken for granted.

As a citizen, one is expected to sacrifice some individual freedoms for the common good. In that sense it is useful to think about the ways in which being an *artistic* citizen may also involve limiting rights to free expression (Bowman 2016: 66). In music projects, a situation where free expression is being curtailed due to care for others in the group might point to a more equitable relationship: one in which artists are acting on their 'responsibilities' as much as their 'rights' (66). This is a form of 'virtue ethics' which sees actions in the moment and *practices* as the place where ethical capacities and ethical character are developed (69 and 70). Bowman also maintains that a practice is 'something living and constantly under interrogation ... Healthy practices involve deliberation and arguments' (74). This resonates strongly with, and has informed, the artistic practices described in this Element which value openness, responsiveness, dialogue, and improvisation, and which, as we will explore, did result in some productive arguments. Acting ethically within musical collaborations also might be instructional for lives outside an arts practice and might indeed exemplify lives lived ethically (75).

A Love Ethic

bell hooks has constructed a framework for productively and ethically exploring difference: the framework of love (2000). hooks' two decades of thinking and writing about power and inequality led to the formation of the 'love ethic' theory. In her early intersectional feminist work, hooks outlined the pervasiveness of 'imperialist, racist, patriarchal society that supports and condones oppression', where personal worth is judged by people's 'personal power, by their ability to oppress others' (hooks 2014: 104). Elsewhere, hooks has elaborated how power in contemporary society is presented as 'normal' rather than 'superior' – indeed this is one of the features of whiteness and the patriarchy, that it has assumed a default position as 'normal' (hooks 1992: 169). For People of Colour, according to hooks, whiteness is perceived as a 'terrorising imposition' (1992: 169).

> Did they understand at all how strange their whiteness appeared in our living rooms, how threatening? Did they journey across the tracks with the same 'adventurous' spirit that other white men carried to Africa, Asia, to those mysterious places they would one day call the 'third world?' Did they come to our houses to meet the Other face-to-face and enact the colonizer role, dominating us on our own turf? (hooks 1992: 170–171)

These questions carry particular ramifications for 'world music', where many of the more famous examples have featured white people travelling to exotic places to record with locals. While our projects all took place in the same city where everyone lived, it still raises uncomfortable questions for a situation in which Toby in travelling from inner Sydney to western Sydney might have appeared as someone dominating others in their own turf.

hooks points to ways to move beyond racist, patriarchal power structures. She states, quoting Gayatri Spivak, that white people in positions of power should 'dehegemonize their position and themselves learn how to occupy the subject position of the other' (1992: 177) and to participate in de-colonisation, 'white artists must embrace and celebrate the concept of non-white subjectivity' (1992: 7. Quoting Christian Walker). 'Subjectivity' is imagined by hooks as fundamentally opposed to 'difference' – the former fully realised personhood, the latter a cultural caricature.

This thinking was the background to hooks' 'love ethic' – a theory to help do the work in dismantling these power structures. hooks describes how bringing a 'love ethic' to our relationships can liberate possibilities for connection and communication. hooks makes the distinction between romantic love, or love as feeling, and a 'love ethic', or 'love as action' (hooks 2000 18–19). Love in this sense is a doing thing, an action and a participation. Love is also political, 'an active force', and the 'primary way we end domination and oppression' (76). It is a way of conquering fear and reaching across difference:

> 'When we are taught that safety lies always with sameness, then difference, of any kind, will appear as a threat. When we choose to love we choose to move against fear – against alienation and separation. The choice to love is a choice to connect – to find ourselves in the other' (93).

These are three sentences that have particular ramifications for our projects – encouraging us to be aware of our fear, reach across difference, and look for personally transformative experiences. Historian and musician Nicole Cherry has also echoed this, stating that 'intentional gender-race relationships will produce new and stronger communities' and encourages artists (and musicians in particular) to 'look beyond their usual kinship circles' (Cherry 2022).

Brydie-Leigh Bartleet has extended hooks' theory of love into the sphere of intercultural popular music making, noting that 'fear is conquered as soon as a guitar comes out of a case, or a pair of drumsticks taken out' (Bartleet 2016: 95). The idea of 'difference' is particularly important for Bartleet's application of this framework, and she writes that 'love across difference' requires a reformulation of the central logic of Western love, transforming a system of possession to one that respects difference and individuality. (100). Bartleet also asks 'how we can we love across difference as intercultural artists, not by reducing identity to notions of sameness, but by the recognition of irreducible differences between us?' (91). This provocation is particularly important for our projects as we seek to both preserve difference and autonomy within a musical project, yet also locate commonalities and produce music that is coherent enough to make sense to a broad audience.

hooks' phrase 'finding oneself in the other' has some ramifications with the Buddhist idea that we should lose a sense of self in order to discover enlightenment (see Tâm 1991). Indeed, Buddhism was a driving force behind hooks' life and philosophies, and is especially apparent in her later work and commentary. In 2015 she said, 'Buddhism continues to inspire me because there is such an emphasis on practice. What are you doing? Right livelihood, right action' (hooks and Yancy 2015). This focus on the doing of things, the practice, has resonances with love as an action, and with Bowman's idea of 'virtue ethics'.

It also connects to Đăng Lan's own philosophy. Buddhism has strongly influenced her approach to music and collaboration and has influenced the individual projects she has been involved with. Đăng Lan says:

> I utilise Buddhist philosophy into the music. For instance, when I play music I have to lose my ego. In Buddhist philosophy, you lessen your ego and you utilise your morality and meditation and wisdom to reach enlightenment, right. This is the same as music. You forget about everything. Only the music. You forget about yourself, and then you achieve something.

The connection between a love ethic and Buddhism is complex and nuanced, but here we can see similarities between the ways in which they provide similar ways of conceptualising self and practice.

A sense of play, sense of humour, and sense of pleasure, are also an important part of a love ethic, and a way of breaking down hierarchies: 'play seems to be essential to any project of critiquing and intervening on a notion of patriarchal authority' (hooks and Hall: 2017: 49) and the 'significance of pleasure' in this context is also important (55). In this, hooks echoes Audre Lorde. Lorde (2007a) has written that 'the erotic' is oppositional to patriarchal, racist society (49). Lorde here conceptualises the erotic as deeply felt pleasure and connection with others (49). For Lorde, like hooks, taking a critical stance in relation to difference is key. 'Too often we pour the energy needed for recognizing and exploring difference into pretending those differences are insurmountable barriers, or that they do not exist at all' (2007b: 108). hooks and Lorde regard the idea of play and pleasure as being instrumental and vital in the deconstruction of white patriarchy. In the discussion of the music projects in Sections 6–8 we highlight moments of play, and also the moments of the project which carried with them particular pleasures for the individual musicians/researchers.

A Love Ethic and a Pop Process

How might a love ethic work when practically applied to making pop music? The answer to that lies both in the ways we relate to each other and the ways we structure the musical material. Care – listening and attending to each other's needs – is important here. Bartleet, referencing Laughter, describes this as a theory of 'micro-kindnesses', in contrast to racist 'micro-aggressions', which might include everyday care for each other and careful listening (Bartleet 2016: 96; Laughter 2014). Similarly, listening to and acting on someone's musical gesture might also be a form of micro-kindness. In this, improvisation can be thought of a series of care-full gestures. A generous spirit to both non-musical activities and to musical ones might make such things possible.

There are also more pragmatic ways in which a 'love ethic' might be applied to the organisation of musical material. This Element explores how un-notated music – in particular developing individual parts through improvisation and jamming – can be a good way to promote connection across difference. This aural method is common in pop, or folk or punk compositional processes, and we think these processes might be a useful way to address the challenges and opportunities presented by employing 'love as action'. Valerie Ross has pointed out that composers who aim to work interculturally must 'unravel challenges in working with different tuning systems, tone and temperament of traditional and western instruments' and to make sure the score permits 'space for performance practices of traditional instruments' (Ross 2016: 434 and 436), not to mention the challenges of working with different cultural backgrounds and expectations. To some degree a pop process has the same challenges – in this case the need for space for different performance practices within an improvisational, or 'jammed', setting – and yet we think that working by ear enables different, and perhaps deeper, forms of collaboration, particularly when the musicians are more comfortable working that way.

Notated music can be a shortcut, a way to address the lack of time that musical projects have, due to busy timetables and restricted budgets. Being able to read a composer's intentions is a quick way to work together. Improvisational writing of parts can be rewarding, but perhaps requires more time. And indeed, how much time cross-cultural projects need will be an important part of the findings of this Element. Other practitioner-scholars have considered this. Campbell and Puruntatameri (2014) have written about a collaboration between Indigenous Australian women from the Tiwi Islands, and Western/white jazz musicians from Sydney. The project was marked by different expectations. For example, Tiwi women wanted 'Westernised' versions of traditional songs, but the jazz musicians preferred songs in the 'old' way. The authors astutely point out: 'We were all attracted to what we perceived to be the other's exoticism' (137). Ultimately a middle ground was found through working by ear and on arrangements through improvisation. The project represented a process of establishing 'impromptu ensemble dynamics' (145), which resonates with our projects, as we will explore later in this Element.

Working aurally and improvisationally does have its own political and musical challenges, not least of which is the desire to please whoever is perceived to be leading the project. Perhaps it is enough to say here that creating music using a pop process might create its own challenges, but also its own opportunities and possibilities for difference in the types of music to be made. We are not suggesting that developing a love ethic through music making can erase the political difficulties caused by centuries of colonialism, but it does provide a productive way of thinking how we can work through it. As Bartleet notes, love cannot 'wipe away the lingering darkness and dangers in colonisation, but rather it can provide a compass for how to step forward' (95).

Music, Politics, and Crossing Borders

Paul Gilroy has written about the ability of music to communicate progressive politics. In particular, Gilroy has looked at the ways in which reggae produced by diasporic Caribbean communities in the UK asserted identity and challenged ethnic ideas of British nationalism in the 1970s and 1980s, helping to usher in broader cultural and political change (Gilroy 2002). In this, Gilroy echoes Jurgen Habermas' idea that music occupies the 'wild part' of the public sphere, before being laundered into the 'serious part' where 'actual political decisions are made' (Habermas in Naerland 2014: 475–476). Importantly, for Gilroy, it is not just music with overtly political lyrics that needs to be considered here, but that analysis should also involve 'consideration of inferred and immanent political positions, specifically of the *musical* forms involved and the social relations in which they are produced and consumed'. This, in turn, necessitates a 'form of analysis capable of moving beyond words and speech' (Gilroy 2002: 266 and 267. Italics in original). Through its powerful ability to communicate struggles and subjectivity, music is able to juxtapose the world 'as it is against the world as the racially subordinated would like it to be . . . this musical culture supplies a great deal of the courage required to go on living in the present' (Gilroy quoted in Frith 1996: 118).

Gilroy is writing about music that emerges from marginalised diasporic communities as a transgressive alternative to dominant national identities, rather than more deliberately manufactured, and institutionally funded, adventures in cross-cultural exploration. However, the relevant point remains that to gauge the political implications of music-making, one needs to look beyond lyrics, to identity, performances, sounds and organisational structures, and that music making often reflects the lived experience of the diversity of a society. Gilroy also notes 'the durability of pop and its capacity to absorb diverse and contradictory elements' (Gilroy 2002: 226). Such diverse and contradictory elements can include reaching beyond racialised borders. Gilroy writes that music 'conjures up and enacts new modes of friendship, happiness and solidarity that are consequent on the overcoming of racial oppression' and that in music 'lines between self and other are blurred' (Gilroy in Frith 1996: 118). Gilroy is imagining here new modes of relationships predominantly between audiences – the wider public – but we would like to extend that for our purposes to include new relationships between musicians.

Music enables the 'construction of community', and is not just illustrative of it (Gilroy 2002: 286). Or to paraphrase Frith, music enacts community identities into being (Frith 1996: 111). For us, music provides an opportunity to play with the group identities we might want to achieve. Through coming together as musicians and playing together, we enact a metaphor of a fairer society.

Aesthetic Implications for Crossing Borders

Some writers (Mitra 2015) have been critical of cross-cultural projects for falling into one of two traps. On the one hand, some projects use a Western art framework and fit other structures into that framework, thus trivialising them as decorative elements, or 'diluting' them (Robinson 2020; Mitra 4). On the other, some projects have different cultural elements working alongside each other, but not in dialogue or with a deeper sense of connection, but rather as a 'superficial collage of cultural-scapes that appear to be precariously glued together like pieces of a jigsaw that do not fit' (Mitra 4). In a search for a 'new', or 'postcolonial', interculturalism, choreographer and dancer Akram Khan has said:

> My aesthetic is driven by a search for common threads and experiences between people, and cultures. I am not as interested in what distinguishes them. This is not at all to deny that differences exist between them, because of course these differences make them culturally unique. But I am keen to find similarities that bind people despite their differences. (Quoted in Cantle 2012: 22)

There is a paradox here. On the one hand cross-cultural art projects need to retain a sense of cultural difference between groups rather than being white-washed. On the other, many, including us, think it is important that such musical projects celebrate commonalities between people of different cultures as a response to reactionary political forces that seek to emphasise and exploit fundamental differences between people.

We will suggest some ways to resolve this paradox later in this Element. Here it is enough to say that this is a tension in cross-cultural music making that needs to be addressed by research. However, we do not necessarily see it as a problem, as Mitra seems to, that the final product might appear collage-like, or glued-together. This might in fact be an appealing aesthetic to some audiences and might hint at ways in which the process has been inclusive, with different groups bringing performance styles together that have not been smoothed out and don't meld easily. Some audiences might expect a certain smoothness of aesthetic, which in music might be represented as Western ideas of equal temperament and rhythmic consistency. Cross-cultural music can sometimes mean a perceived messiness of aesthetic, yet this messiness or textural complexity may well be indicative of a democratic process as well as being musically interesting to many.

Democracy and Music Making

Another useful conceptual framework for thinking about cross-cultural collaboration is democracy. Adlington and Buch have outlined ways in which music making can 'model democracy' through the negotiation of relationships between musicians or between composers and musicians: 'music is an arena for many kinds of decision making, and thus for the negotiation of power' and one of these types of decision making is democratic (Adlington and Buch 2020: 9). They also point out the ways in which the musical material itself can embody ideas of democracy, for instance composers might represent democracy through competing multiple, polyphonous voices, and jazz performers might represent this through the equitable distribution of soloing (10).

Both these conceptions of musical democracy have critically guided our music making. The projects discussed here attempt to remove hierarchies and democratise decision-making processes, and they also allow space for the expression of multiple voices. Sometimes these voices provide a messy, tangled texture; on other occasions individual voices rise up out of the texture to be heard, and then sink back in. On *Songs from Northam Avenue*, compare for instance the dense soundscape of Chapel and Dellwood with the emergence of the đàn tranh as a singular soaring voice in the last couple of minutes of Correctional Complex. As in political democracy, there are many voices that sometimes compete to be heard, and sometimes find harmony. All three projects discussed here have a certain wildness or raggedness that we find in keeping with a democratic aesthetic and a democratic process.

While popular music often showcases the talents of individual virtuosos (Adlington and Buch 2020: 12), it also has a particular history of the collaborative ensemble, especially the small-format, three-to-five-piece band. One of the reasons for the appeal of ensembles such as Radiohead, Talking Heads, The Slits, and De La Soul, to name but a few famous examples, is that much of the pleasure of being a fan of the group is located in the sense that one is listening to several highly individualistic performances combining into a satisfying whole. What gives them a democratic allure is the feeling of listening to something with many voices. The making of much popular music since the 1960s has a particular history of, and relationship with, democracy that is beyond the scope of this Element. Let us say here though that a popular music democratic method and aesthetic is important to our projects and which our projects test out and explore.

Co-produced Research in Other Disciplines

For many Indigenous communities historically, 'research is a dirty word' (Smith 1999: 1), with anthropologists regarded as an extension of the colonial apparatus. As a response to this problem, ethnomusicology has deepened its sense of collaboration and research 'subjects' have increasingly become researchers themselves. Katelyn Barney's edited collection on collaborative ethnomusicology between Indigenous and non-Indigenous Australians suggests ways we might do music research within a culture still dealing with the toxic legacy of colonialism. Barney and Proud (2014) write that collaborative ethnomusicological research represents an important way to improve scholarly outcomes and real relations between Indigenous and non-Indigenous Australians (83 and 91). They see collaborative relations as an opportunity for 'the mutual search for answers' that allows for the 'unsticking' of relationships between Indigenous and non-Indigenous people' (85). Research in these areas becomes a 'contact zone', a place of asymmetrical power relations, where self and other are negotiated (86. See also James Clifford 2008). Somerville (2014) writes that this contact zone might be called the 'discomfort zone': a place of productive difference (17). Mackinlay and Chalmers (2014) write that for Western researchers 'fixing' and 'knowing' 'the other' perpetuates the violence of colonialism, and that all participants in research should be regarded as relational rather than fixed (65).

Such theorising has echoes for practice-based research and music making that involves people from different cultural backgrounds coming together. Musicians, and artists in general, know the importance of being in the 'discomfort zone' when creating and making. It is often when one is out of one's comfort zone that interesting things happen and artistic advances are made.

However, in situations which involve power imbalances, the challenge is to make the discomfort zone a place that, while artistically uncomfortable, is safe, nourishing and productive on a personal/individual level.

Similarly, we find the idea of 'unsticking' relationships via collaborative research an exciting one. Entering into a collaborative artistic relationship with someone from a very different background, who uses a very different musical language, requires you to unstick yourself from previous ways of making music in order to enter into a new way of doing things. This idea of unsticking connects to the earlier discussion of the Buddhist negotiation of self, as well as hooks' thoughts on self and other, and overcoming fear. We can extend this idea to include our fear, as musicians, of being unstuck from our background and training and cast adrift. (Although it is also important to preserve performance practices that are both the result of years of training and experience, and might be vulnerable to being marginalised or lost.) Musicians might usefully take a sense of 'unstuckness' with them once a project ends. Working cross-culturally does not just bring people from different cultures together, it changes them and opens up new opportunities for future work.

Regarding one's collaborators as relational and un-fixed seems important, especially given the long history of Indigenous and non-European musicians being regarded as 'pure', fixed, unchanging, even 'primitive' (Fabian 1983; Torgovnik 1990). One of the reasons that non-white/Western cultures have been treated as 'spice' is that they are often regarded as having unchanging traditions. It is very easy to walk into a project with certain ideas of what a musician brings to it, especially when that musician has been employed in order to bring a specific style to a project. Invariably though, especially given the time and opportunity, surprising things occur. As an example of this, at the first performance of *Songs from Northam Avenue*, at a front yard in Bankstown for the Sydney Festival, the sound system suddenly failed just as we were about to launch into the first song. To fill time and to retain the attention of the audience, Alex Hadchiti performed an impromptu medley of Beatles songs acoustically on the oud, delightfully playing with audience expectations about the repertoire of an Arabic musician.

Examples of collaborative research in history are also useful for our purposes. Especially examples from local, community histories, and histories of local music making. Work in these areas has shown how involving local community members as co-producers of research leads not just to better histories, but to positive group identity building (Brown et al. 2020). In two examples that are close to home for this Element, being based in Huddersfield, UK, the Soundsystems Culture project has revealed and celebrated the richness of the town's history of reggae, while a project on the history of bhangra has shown the vitality of South Asian musical forms in the area (Huxtable 2014; Sahota 2014).

Here, we extend the idea of co-produced research into songs, recordings, and concerts. Songwriting and music making in fact create new opportunities for doing co-produced research. While the popular music industry has certainly participated in the replication and reinforcement of colonial power structures it also carries possibilities through its emphasis on collaboration. The term 'co-songwriter', or 'musician', suggests different relationships than does 'co-author'. It is also an embodied method of doing research, where bodily and oral knowledge is privileged. These elements prioritise expertise that comes from lived experience rather than institutional recognition. A key part of colonial supremacy has been the privileging of European constructions of knowledge that grew out of the post-Renaissance tradition of rationalism, objectivity, and the scientific method, over other forms of knowledge, especially Indigenous knowledge (see Lorde 2019). If mindful about the power and economic structures, collaborative practice-based research has the potential to lead to expansive and novel research outputs.

Practice-based research, alongside new methods of ethnomusicology and critical ethnography, can offer an alternative to the 'white settler colonial privilege to know about the music of others' (Mackinlay and Chalmers 2014: 74). Rather than employing researchers to try to find out something about the music of others, embodied research aims to create new knowledge via a shared practice, with all participants being co-creators of knowledge. The projects written about here represent examples of co-produced research. All participants – whether composers or performers – are co-authors of the research outputs (the concerts or the recordings).

Thinking about music and research in these ways also can lead to thinking about musical relationships in general. People you play music with can, and maybe should, be considered co-creators of that music. That stands in contrast to the anachronistic ways in which popular music copyright works, where 'songwriters' are often credited as the authors, while 'performers' are not. This occurs even when performers write their own parts and those parts become integral to the song. Considering all musicians involved as equal creators of knowledge, as research collaborators rather than 'session musicians', opens up new ways of doing the business of pop music.

However, returning to Robinson's (2020) ideas of 'fit' outlined earlier on, it is also important to consider who initiates and devises the musical or research project. Some scholars have said it is simply not enough for non-Indigenous people to ask Indigenous people to be involved with projects; rather they need to be devised together (Barney and Proud 2014: 93; Robinson 2020).The projects that we write about here were all devised differently, and in fact these projects represent a process of working through issues of power and control. *Songs from*

Northam Avenue and *I Felt the Valley Lifting* were initiated by Toby and the lyrics and vocal melodies of the songs were written before the other collaborators were involved, and Toby paid the musicians to play on the record, and pursued and organised the concert opportunities. In *Two Sounds Gliding*, however, Lan and Toby started the project together from scratch and were employed and paid as equal artists by an external source. This less hierarchical starting point set a standard for the subsequent stages of the project. Both Lan and Toby pursued performance opportunities that extend from Toby's contacts (arts festivals, pub gigs) to Lan's contacts (Tết performances at Buddhist temples) and had equal billing in performance and on the recordings. While all three projects involved long periods of musical collaboration, the structural and economic concerns of the projects did affect the process. Throughout the case studies we will discuss not just the creation of musical material, but also the ways in which the musical projects were commissioned, organised and financed, and how this affected the sense of equality.

This section has discussed scholarship from a variety of disciplines that has been instrumental in developing our framework. This framework has informed the ways in which our music projects have taken place, and also has allowed us to critically evaluate those projects. The scholars mentioned here have grappled with the politics, ethics, and aesthetics of relationships, of artistic practice, of cross-cultural music and co-produced research. Many have pointed out the challenges inherent to cross-cultural artistic projects due to the distribution of power and privilege in what is still a highly patriarchal, racist, and capitalist society. However, many have also been cautiously hopeful about the possibilities of music making to be inclusive, democratic, and diverse. We are mindful of the potential for our musical projects to perpetuate white supremacist ideas of 'spice' and 'fit', but also of how ideas of 'artistic citizenship', a 'love ethic', and 'co-produced research' might be usefully deployed to challenge hegemonies. We also hope that our lived experiences of working and playing together can provide practice-centered evidence to contribute to this broader ethical discussion, as we will discuss in the coming sections on the individual projects. Before that, however, we will briefly outline our own backgrounds and biographies.

5 Collaborators' Backgrounds

In order to understand the context of the three collaborations, it is necessary to briefly outline each author's musical and cultural background, their performance histories, and their particular expertise on various instruments. In keeping with the idea of autoethnography and 'at home ethnomusicology', we turn the gaze on ourselves (Nooshin 2014; Nettl 1995).

Seyed MohammadReza Beladi and the Music of Bushehr

I am a musician and a researcher, originally from Iran, but have lived in England since 2011. My research has been mainly focussed on the music of Bushehr, a port city in southern Iran. My primary instrument is the dammam (drum) but I also play neyanban (bagpipe) and ney (flute). My main musical output has been with Leymer Folk Music and Dance Group of Bushehr, with whom I am director, composer, and performer.[8] Leymer have performed extensively in Asia and Europe, including at major music and arts festivals. I have also worked with music students at the University of Huddersfield, where the students performed with a combination of different instruments, including from Bushehr and some Western musical instruments. 'The Evolution of Music in the Multicultural Society of Bushehr' is the title of my Master's thesis and my PhD research focussed on the history and role of the neyanban. 'The Anthropology of Bushehr Music' was the title of a research project I conducted for the Iranian Cultural Heritage Organization in 1996. My latest work is a book titled *Music of Bushehr and Its Origins*, published in Iran in 2021.

In understanding the musical and cultural language that I have brought to the projects discussed in this Element, it is important to outline the significance of Bushehr and its music. Bushehr – by virtue of its proximity to Africa and the Indian subcontinent – has developed vernacular musical traditions that are somewhat different to classical Persian music and are distinctly multicultural. Bushehr is a port city, located on the peninsula in the south-west of Iran and on the northern coast of the Persian Gulf. The Bushehr Peninsula was one of the most important ports of the Elamite civilisation (3200 BC–539 BC) called Liyan (Edwards, Hammond, and Sollberger 1975). Over the past centuries, social developments in Bushehr have resulted in music containing cultural elements from other nations due to assimilation and blending. The multicultural milieu resulting from the presence of different ethnic groups in Bushehr over the past centuries is an important aspect of Bushehr's social and cultural situation, which has also played a key role in its musical structure. The presence of different ethnic groups such as Africans, Arabs, and Persians, as well as the trade and cultural relations between Bushehr and other nations such as the Indian subcontinent, and African and Arab countries, led to the emergence of a multicultural and diverse musical culture in Bushehr. The music of Bushehr has different branches that are used in the daily life of the people with different rituals. The most important of these branches are the sailors' songs (work music), musical rituals of Zar for healing people suffering from mental and psychological problems, festive music, and religious music.

---

[8] www.leymer.info.

The neyanban is one of the most important musical instruments in southern Iran and Bushehr. The two main components of this instrument are the 'ney' or pipes (also known as the handle or chanter) and the 'anban' or bag. When the pipes are set into the frame, it is called the 'dasteh'. This wind instrument is part of the global bagpipe family. In fact, it was a key influence on the development of the bagpipes of the British Isles, brought by the Romans 2,000+ years ago (Beladi 2023: 58). By blowing on the bag and transferring air to the pipes, the instrument can produce seven different pitches based on the musical tone patterns used by neyanban players. The history of this instrument in Iran dates to the first half of the second millennium BC (Harper, Aruz, and Tallon 1992; Beladi 2023). Since then, the physical structure and musical repertoire have also changed in accordance with social and cultural evolutions and the changes that have been made to its status and function.

The ney is a woodwind instrument and is found in both Iranian classical and folk traditions. In the past it was played in many parts of Iran, including Bushehr, as an instrument of the shepherds and developed local variations. The folk way of playing is slightly different from the classical way of playing. The folk method is called 'ney-e labi' (i.e. the ney played with the 'lab' or lips) sometimes known as 'shepherd's ney', while the classical method is called 'haft-band ney (seven loops) or 'ney-e dandooni' (played with the teeth). In Bushehr, the ney has been used to accompany local non-metrical songs such as Sharveh (Beladi 2021). I play the ney as it is in Iranian classical music.

The dammam is a type of drum, a cylindrical percussion instrument with two sides. The dammam is mainly used in Bushehr in Islamic religious ceremonies called 'Senj-o-Dammam'. In the Senj-o-Dammam ceremony, the player of the dammam traditionally uses a stick in their right hand to beat the drum while playing with the other hand without a stick. Senj-o-Dammam is a musical ceremony performed at the beginning of the Bushehr mourning ritual. This ceremony is performed with seven drums called dammam, eight cymbals called 'senj' and a horn called 'booq'. However, the dammam or similar drums are also used in other rituals, such as the sailors' rituals and music and 'Zar ceremonies. It seems likely that this instrument has an African origin and is a remnant of rituals formerly performed by African immigrants or slaves (Beladi 2021).

While we were interested and excited to be fusing different cultural and musical elements in the twenty-first century, it is important to note that this is not new. In fact, the same thing has been happening for years in multicultural societies like Bushehr, whose music is the result of the interaction and fusion of different cultures. My music is the folk music of Bushehr, but this itself is the result of centuries of cultural mixing.

Đăng Lan and Vietnamese Music

I was born in Vietnam. I studied literature and philosophy in Saigon. I also studied traditional Vietnamese performance styles, learning instruments such as the đàn bầu (one-string monochord), đàn tranh (sixteen-string zither), and sinh tien (wood and coin clappers). I also studied singing and learnt modern western styles of music as well as traditional Vietnamese styles. I sang both styles of music at the Queen Bee club in Saigon, and sometimes I performed on đàn bầu and đàn tranh at special community events, or in schools.

In 1975 I was forced to leave during the War and the Fall of Saigon. After a dangerous boat voyage and a temporary stay in a camp in Hong Kong, I was granted asylum in Australia. I was part of the first wave of Vietnamese refugees that came to Australia as a result of the war. My first place of residence was the East Hills Migrant Hostel in Sydney's south-west.

My husband and I owned and ran a Vietnamese restaurant in downtown Sydney. However, I remained a highly active recording and touring musician, actor, and dancer. I have appeared regularly as a musician and dancer in concerts around Sydney and interstate. I have performed regularly for the Vietnamese community and at multicultural festival events such as the Festival of Asian Music and Dance. I teach đàn tranh and đàn bầu and in fact I have played these instruments more since coming to Australia, as Vietnamese people in Australia miss that kind of music. I have toured to the USA, Canada, and Noumea. I have translated and recited poems for the Australian PEN club, performed in broadcasting for ABC, SBS Television, Channel 7, and have worked as a presenter and a singer on SBS radio from 1977 to 1990 and the Vietnamese programme on radio 2MBS FM, and as a voiceover artist for government and commercial advertising.

The đàn tranh is known in English as a Vietnamese zither or dulcimer, closely related to the Chinese guzheng. It usually has sixteen strings – sometimes eighteen or twenty-one – spread out flat on a wooden frame and tuned to five repeating notes. Each string is separated by a moveable wooden bridge. On one side of the bridge the strings are plucked, and on the other side they are bent by a semi-tone or more to give access to extra notes. Melodies can be plucked out, but sweeping harp-like sounds are also common. The đàn tranh is seen regularly in Vietnamese classical, folk, pop, and experimental music, or accompanying poetry recitations. It can be played solo or in ensembles, and traditionally it has been played by both men and women.

The đàn bầu is a special and typical instrument of Vietnam. It has one string, set on a long wooden soundboard. At one end the string is attached to a flexible stem which can bend the string. The player uses a long bamboo stick to pluck the string while it resonates against the side of the hand – producing a harmonic note. This note is then bent with the stem. Modern đàn bầus have a guitar pick up and are plugged into an amp.[9]

Old people, old-fashioned people, do not like their daughters to listen to a man playing the đàn bầu, because the sound is so touching. They don't want their daughters to be seduced and fall in love with the đàn bầu musicians because most of the musicians are very poor. Traditional people, like my parents a long time ago, also didn't like women to play the đàn bầu because it is so sad. It sounds like a human voice. If you play it you become negative, not positive. My mother was not happy with me playing đàn bầu. Even my husband doesn't like it. On the first day of lunar new year I was playing it and he said 'Stop it! It brings bad luck for the whole year.' So if I play đàn bầu I have to play happy songs, not sad songs.

Toby Martin and Western Indie/Folk Rock

I am a musician and academic from Australia. I am of Anglo-Celtic and Central European–Jewish origin and both my grandparents and parents migrated to Australia just after World War Two. I grew up middle class in inner-city Melbourne and Canberra, but have lived mostly in Sydney as an adult. My musical practice is within the field of indie rock. This is a broad genre that grew out of punk in the 1980s and 1990s and sets itself as distinct from classic rock through its emphasis on nuance, expressivity, and lo-fi recording practices, rather than the glossier, virtuosic sound of classic rock. More recently, this influence has been complemented by a growing interest in folk music.

I am a songwriter, singer, and guitarist. I have written and recorded nine albums, five of which have been with the band Youth Group with whom I have toured extensively. My lyrics have an observational quality – with songs that emphasise place and character – and my melodies seek a plaintive yet well-ordered melodicism. As a guitarist, I use primarily non-standard tunings, a practice that has emerged from the pioneering work of punk and post-punk bands like the Velvet Underground and Sonic Youth, as well as folk guitarists such as Joni Mitchell and Martin Carthy. Non-standard tunings can create arrangements which, while often being drone-like, also have a complex harmonic sense, with ghostly overhanging notes, while remaining direct and energetic pop songs. It can also liberate songwriting from an overreliance on harmonic movement, as minimal chord progressions in different tunings are rich and interesting even when staying on one or two chords, and from overly

---

[9] The sound of a *đàn bầu* is similar to that of a theremin.

complicated fingering patterns, as small fingering moves can create big changes.

In the last decade, I have developed a practice which focusses on two elements. Firstly, lyrics that are strongly rooted in specific places and use everyday language to evoke detail and character. This practice emerged from my work with Aboriginal country musicians, primarily Gomeroi elder and singer Uncle Roger Knox. In 2013 I undertook a songwriting residency at Campbelltown Arts Centre, in western Sydney, where Uncle Roger and collaborators wrote an album's worth of lyrics based around Roger's life for his album. Secondly, collaborations with musicians from diverse cultural backgrounds. This practice has emerged from meeting and working with people like Đăng Lan and MomammadReza Beladi – and indeed the experience of getting to know them and their music has changed not just the way I think about music and collaboration, but the way I think about friendship and connection.

I am also a historian of popular music. My research has looked particularly at country music in Australia, and what country music songwriting and performance practices can tell us about bigger patterns of history. Country music songwriting is often based around narrative storytelling and evokes a strong sense of place, which has echoes in my own songwriting practice that is the subject of this Element.

6 Project 1: *Songs from Northam Avenue* (2013–2017)

Musicians

Maroun Azar	mijwiz
Cameron Emerson-Elliott	guitar
Alex Hadchiti	oud, keyboard
Zoe Hauptmann	double bass
Đăng Lan	đàn bầu, đàn tranh, teacup, and coin percussion
Mohammed Lelo	qanun
Toby Martin	guitar, vocals
Matthew Steffen	electric bass
Bree van Reyk	drums
Anh Linh Pham	đàn tranh
Phong Phu	đàn bầu

(**Note:** Anh Linh and Phu only appeared in the first performance; on the album and in later concerts they were replaced by Đăng Lan).

Producers
Bree van Reyk
Toby Martin

Recording engineer
Bob Scott

Composers
Toby Martin

Results
One album. Concert performances at Sydney Festival, Carriageworks, Casula Powerhouse and National Gallery of Victoria.

Financing
Urban Theatre Projects, or Utp commissioned Toby for the original songwriting and paid a flat weekly fee. For the recording, Toby paid musicians directly from his own finances as a one-off fee. The engineer and studio were paid both through Toby's finances, and through an internal research grant from the University of Huddersfield. For the concerts, all musicians (including Toby) received the same fee. Songwriting royalties for the recording go to Toby, performance royalties go to the musicians.

Songwriting and Background (Toby)

In 2013, I (Toby) was commissioned by Urban Theatre Projects (Utp) to be an artist in residence for their Practice and Participate project. Utp are an innovative arts company based in Bankstown, a suburb in south-western Sydney with a markedly culturally diverse population, notably with Vietnamese and Arabic backgrounds.[10] Utp have forged strong connections with these communities, both as artists and as audiences. Since World War Two Bankstown has been a place which many new migrants to Australia have called home. These include my own father and grandparents who lived there after migrating from Europe to Sydney in 1949.

For Practice and Participate, I set up in local residents' front yards in order to write songs. The first location was an abandoned house on Northam Avenue, but it was directly across the road from David and his daughter Catherine, who effectively functioned as my hosts. David has Anglo-Scottish ancestry

---

[10] According to the SBS Census Explorer, 55 per cent of Bankstown residents speak a language other than English at home (20 per cent Arabic, 10 per cent Vietnamese) and the predominant birthplace (other than Australia) is Vietnam. www.sbs.com.au/news/creative/census-explorer/xtjxeqygs, accessed 1 February 2023.

and has lived in the same house since he was born there in the 1930s. The second location I was given was out the front of a mixed business store, on a busy corner in Bankstown. The business was owned by Michael of Arabic-Islamic background, who had moved to Sydney from Lebanon in the 1980s.

All parties were extremely hospitable. Meals and coffee were shared and conversations that I had with Michael, David, and Catherine inevitably found their ways into the lyrics of the songs I was writing. Dreams in German was an attempt to encapsulate aspects of David's life in a snapshot. Olive Tree came from a conversation with Michael about playing the national anthem at the soccer. There were also interactions with passers-by, for instance a traditional Vietnamese melody sung by one man became the basis of 'Lim's Song'.

The physical locations also fed into the writing of the songs. Northam Avenue was wide, quiet, peaceful, reflective. The nature strips clipped, the gutters smooth. Small planes from Bankstown airport went overhead. Such landscapes inspired the song Bankstown Airport. Michael's shop on the other hand was surrounded by busy traffic and constant friends and customers coming and going. This more frantic feeling fed into songs like 'Chapel and Dellwood' and 'Olive Tree'. On lunch breaks, I would go up to Bankstown shopping centre where the air was filled with a multiphony of sounds – pumping Arabic beats from cars, a busker playing the Chinese Erhu, the Vietnamese fish and fruit and vegetable shops thronging with languages.

The songs were inspired by the people, the locations, and the sounds of Bankstown. A diverse, bustling hubbub. It was also inspired by a place where people from many different backgrounds harmoniously co-existed and formed a community based on geographic proximity. This was in contrast to the ways in which Bankstown had been represented by Sydney tabloid media. New migrants have long been vilified in the Australian media, and frequently publications such as the *Daily Telegraph* depict western Sydney as a place where migrant cultures become ghettoised and criminalised (Markus 1994; Blair 2014). Western Sydney has often been presented as Sydney's 'other'. As Michael Mohammad Ahmad has noted, migrant cultures from western Sydney have been under-represented in the media as valuable contributors to society, and over-represented in terms of crime:

> 'There are always news reports of shootings and stabbings in the western suburbs, and often these are connected to the perpetrator's cultural backgrounds and religions. I have heard the words "Asian", "Vietnamese", "Lebanese", "Pacific Islander", "Middle Eastern" and "Muslim" come up way too many times' (Ahmad: 2013).

In the first two decades of the twenty-first century, this general trend has been focussed into a specific Islamophobia, which was intensified in the wake of 9/11 and the so-called 'War on Terror'. At the time of my residency – in 2013 – one of the biggest stories in the national and local media was about young Arabic-Islamic men being recruited into Isis and travelling to Syria. Many of these young men came from south-western Sydney. The media's focus on this story – which involved a relatively small number of people – was yet another example of the ways in which People of Colour from western Sydney have been represented. This issue is the background to the song 'Olive Tree'.

My experience of Bankstown was starkly opposite to this. A place where many cultures existed alongside each other, and most importantly interacted with each other. The idea of ghettoisation of migrant cultures that Sydney media often likes to deploy was drastically overstated, serving instead to illustrate how isolated some aspects of majority Anglo, English-speaking Sydney were from the cultural diversity of Sydney. The music and the musicians on *Songs from Northam Avenue* were designed as a direct response to this – a counter-narrative.

Musical Arrangements (Toby)

Hoping to represent Bankstown musically as well as lyrically, I began contacting Arabic and Vietnamese cultural organisations, seeking out the details of musicians from these communities. This led me to meet and work with Alex Hadchiti, Mohammed Lelo, and Maroun Azar, all of Arabic background, and Anh Linh Pham, Phong Phu, and Đăng Lan of Vietnamese background. I also invited several musicians who I had worked with before – Cameron Emerson-Elliott, Matthew Steffen, and Bree van Reyk. In fact, Bree also took on a key artistic role and became a co-producer of the album.

In the several months leading up to recording the album in 2015, rehearsals took place in two stages. Regular one-on-one rehearsals between the other musicians and me, and then an intensive three-day period with the band all together. The first stage of rehearsals took place mostly in people's houses in inner west and western Sydney. Rehearsal methods were responsive to individual needs and preferences. For instance, Alex Hadchiti and I sat together and worked up the songs without listening to demos and planning beforehand. However, Lan preferred listening to demos of the songs on CD beforehand and working out a rough sense of parts before playing together. Once this had happened, Lan and I met once a week in the two months leading up to the album recording. This length of time was important, particularly as the combination of Western and Vietnamese instrumentation presented many more difficulties than other combinations (as we shall discuss later). Food was shared during jam sessions too – Iranian dates with Alex, vermicelli and international spaghetti with Lan. Mohammed Lelo, the qanun player, had young children, a busy work schedule, and was more limited in his time. He was also more virtuosic and more experienced in jamming and improvising in a variety of musical contexts, including jazz bands. Consequently, Mohammed wrote his own parts once the full band met together for a few days of rehearsals directly prior to recording the album.

These jam sessions also produced unexpected directions, as preconceptions became unstuck. For instance, I originally approached Alex because he played oud, but during the first jam session he turned on his Yamaha PSR-A2000 keyboard and started playing along to the songs, suggesting some pre-programmed beats, piano and organ sounds, and sampled Arabic sounds. This was closer to Alex's performance practice – playing solo keyboard in marathon three-hour sets at local Lebanese restaurants and at weddings. In wanting to capture a truly 'Arabic' sound I had presumed what that might be and was attracted to instruments like the oud because of their, for me, exotic flavours. A Yamaha keyboard was more known, and, I assumed, more Western. But it was clear that the digital keyboard was, for Alex, as much part of his cultural background and performance culture as the oud, and so that became a key part of the album's sound (e.g. the tracks 'Central City Plaza' or 'Minto Mall').[11]

While there were important differences between the one-on-one rehearsals, there were key similarities too. Individual parts were all written by the performers themselves through an aural, improvised process. Very little direction was offered by me, but rather arrangement sessions used extended time and a careful process of listening to create musically coherent and interesting parts. Another constant was that musicians brought their performance styles and cultures to the project. Methods of playing from other performance practices were transposed onto these indie-folk song skeletons. For instance, Alex Hadchiti and Mohammed Lelo brought a method of call and response to the project, ghosting the vocal melody in the spaces between phrases. Đăng Lan would play pentatonic-based riffs that would not be out of place in traditional Vietnamese music (i.e. the intro of 'Spring Feeling'). Sometimes, although this happened less, Alex, Mohammed and Lan would provide a harmonic bed for the songs.

---

[11] In fact, this happened again in 2019 during rehearsals for the Sounding Out Refugee Stories project in Amman, Jordan. I was hoping to work with a qanun player, but the musical director of the project Mohammed Zitari preferred the sampled qanun sounds from his digital keyboard. Western musicians can easily fetishise supposedly 'traditional' styles, while those who play such styles have moved on and are finding ways to make traditional styles live and breathe in a modern world, and also find ways to be economically smarter (as a band leader it is much cheaper to do it all yourself on a keyboard rather than pay multiple musicians).

This was akin to the Western idea of guitar or piano chords as accompaniment, yet was something more foreign to the Vietnamese and Arabic players.

The *Songs from Northam Avenue* project had notable limitations, with the songs being written before collaboration occurred. However, the limitations provided an opportunity and a framework to be inventive with the combining of musical cultures within existing songs. For this project we created a musical world where performance practices were re-contextualised and allowed to sit alongside each other, their differences marked and transparent, the stitches showing rather than seamless.

Matching Sounds (Toby and Lan)

On a technical level, while it was relatively easy, in terms of pitch and harmony, to make the guitar work with the oud and the qanun, it proved much trickier to match the guitar with the đàn tranh and đàn bầu. Lan says:

> When I first heard the songs, I couldn't believe it! At that time I didn't think I had a musical attitude that would work with a Western style. I didn't know anything about that. So when Toby gave me the tape with his songs, I talked to myself, I said 100 per cent I couldn't do it, I couldn't combine my instruments with Western styles. But after listening I found that I could improvise. I felt free to improvise, to play with the sound, to match with it.[12]

The reasons for why it eventually worked – how we made the sounds match – are various and diverse. As the following exchange between us shows, the explanations range from Lan's Buddhist philosophy, with emphasis on karma, to more technical explanations about the structure of the songs. We are keen not to privilege one explanation over another, which is why we present this as a conversation:

T: So, you thought 'oh this is never going to work' but then something happened to make you think it could work, so do you remember what that was? What made you think it could work?

---

[12] As mentioned in the prologue, Lan had experience in performing both Western songs and Vietnamese songs since the 1970s in Vietnam; however, she had not tried to play Western styles on Vietnamese instruments. As Barley Norton notes, musical expression underwent many changes and modernisation from the late colonial period in Vietnam, with composers, songwriters, and musicians interested in devising forms and performance styles that brought in Western influences, yet were also distinctively Vietnamese. One of the most distinctive blendings of 'east' and 'west' was *cai luong* which was made up of two ensembles: one playing traditional repertoire on Vietnamese instruments, the other playing newly composed incidental music on Western instruments. Western popular music, harmony and phrasing also had a strong influence on Vietnamese songwriters, whose new music had a strongly sentimental and romantic flavour (2009: 27). However, in Lan's experience, she had not specifically tried to match Vietnamese instruments with Western styles.

L: I don't know why! I just listened to your music and then I felt something similar. I felt like I had heard that somewhere before in my mind. It felt familiar with my style.

T: Because it was familiar, because of other Western music you had heard? Or . . .?

L: No, the first time, and other times, that I listened to other Western music I didn't have that feeling. But I don't know why when I listened to your music . . . maybe that is karma. Maybe karma between you and me.

T: It might be karma. It might also be that I don't use very many chords in the songs.

L: Not too many chord changes. That's why it is suitable with đàn tranh and đàn bầu, because their scale is tight, not like Western styles.

T: And with my guitar I tend to just have two chords, or something, and well the guitar is kind of pentatonic, well you can make it pentatonic . . .

L: Yeah you're right. In your music you don't change much, that's why it is easier to follow you.

T: Yeah, and then it's like layering, you layer things on top . . .

A sense of karmic connection was important for the project in terms of establishing trust between Lan and Toby. However, there was still some work to do in terms of making the instruments fit. In order to find a part on the đàn tranh that would work, Lan had to change the tuning. The đàn tranh is a pentatonic instrument, with five main notes that can be bent approximately a semi-tone in either direction:

> The usual tuning for North Vietnamese styles is G/A/C/D/E repeated, while for south Vietnamese traditional music it is G/B/C/D/F. The tuning stays in the frame of five main notes.
>
> For the *Songs from Northam Avenue* project, it was necessary for me to find the key to match by changing the tuning on the đàn tranh – for instance in the songs in F♯ major (i.e. 'Correctional Complex') it was necessary to change the E to D♯. Sometimes it wasn't always necessary to tune but to change the pitch by bending individual strings. Sometimes I didn't need to tune, I could press. I could borrow. If I wanted to play D♯, I could push the D string so it came up to D♯.

This presented particular challenges for performances. The đàn tranh took some time to tune, and had to be done by ear rather than with a digital tuner, and so Lan needed to bring three different instruments for the concerts, each one in a different tuning. The đàn tranh is also a very delicate instrument. Small bumps can throw the tuning out completely or cause the strings to be dislodged. Backstage at the *Songs from Northam Avenue* shows would be three đàn tranhs, carefully tuned, labelled and ready to substitute during the concert. This was not the case for Lan's performances of traditional material where she was able to play several songs in the same tuning on the same instrument.

Lan did not only change her tuning, but she also changed what she played. In particular, she often changed her instrument to harmonic accompaniment, rather than a lead instrument.

> What I play is quite different. When I play in Vietnamese style, mostly I play solo, I play the main note, the song. I play the melody. But when I play with Toby, I play the harmony.
>
> It's hard to play a Western-style melody. There are not enough notes. So I have to play harmony. But sometimes there are some notes that match with the đàn bầu or đàn tranh. So I can play the melody. But it has to stay within a five-note scale.

The use of the đàn tranh as a melodic lead instrument can be heard in the introduction to 'Spring Feeling'. The use of the đàn tranh as a harmonic instrument can be heard in Chapel and Dellwood, although not as chords, but rather as a single repeated note or arpeggiated accompaniment.

Having only one string, a high pitch range, and not much sustain, the đàn bầu is invariably a lead instrument. However, its tuning still needs to change:

> 'You can only change half notes. Otherwise you need different strings, and when you buy the string you have to tell the shop you need A, D, or C string. So a C string you can tune up to C# or down to B; that's it. From D to E is too tight.'

It took some experimentation to find the right key for the songs featuring the đàn bầu and Lan needed two đàn bầus for performances and for recording.

All in all, Lan did some fairly radical things with her instruments – things that are unusual within the context of Vietnamese traditional music and certainly had never been tried by Lan before. She changed the tuning of the đàn tranh, moving away from the two traditional sets of tuning, and she transformed the đàn tranh into a harmonic instrument. Not only was this an exploratory way of using the instrument, there was no training or guide on how to do it. Lan's education did not cover collaborating across cultures, nor mine for that matter, but had to be worked out through exploration and experimentation.

> We do not know these things from learning from a teacher. From a teacher I only learnt the basics of music. But day by day and year by year the more I experienced, the more I found out. We have to find out ourselves. Sometimes

you don't understand the whole of your capacity. You don't know until you do it. And when things come, and something comes to you, something happens to you and then you have to do it and you have to think.

Once the relationship between the guitar, the đàn tranh, and the đàn bầu was established, it was relatively easy to match that cluster of sounds with the oud and qanun, as they can both be played as chromatic instruments. What was apparent from the moment this first occurred in the big rehearsal was how special this triangulation of sounds – Arabic, Vietnamese, and Western – was. Certainly none of the musicians had been a part of such an ensemble and they were enthused about its novelty. As Mohammed Lelo said in a short film we made about the project: 'it's the first time' this combination had occurred (Meredith 2017).

Recording (Toby and Lan)

The recording process for *Songs from Northam Avenue* also saw a combination of culturally distinct processes being employed. While I and the other musicians with a Western rock/contemporary background – Cameron Emerson-Elliott, Matthew Steffen – were more used to overdubbing and layering take after take, Alex, Mohammed and Lan were more comfortable with live recording. As Lan says: 'I prefer to record live. I don't like to be alone, or separated. I like to feel like I am one of them.'

This also corresponded with engineer Bob Scott and producer Bree van Reyk's experience with and preference for live recording, due to their work in experimental and classical music. The result was many more 'live' takes than in my experience of recording indie rock records; in fact, the song 'Olive Tree' has no overdubs at all, except for the backing vocals. But, conversely, there are also more overdubs and layering than would normally be the case for Lan, Alex, or Mohammed Hadchiti, or Lelo. In this way, the recording process itself was representative of a middle ground, or meeting place. Also, the overdubs provided a place where some of the sonic properties of the instruments were pushed, and the idea of bringing culturally grounded performances to the record was loosened. For instance, Lan ran her đàn tranh through a distortion pedal and the result could be mistaken for a guitarist using a whammy bar (i.e. the outro of 'Correctional Complex').

Outcomes and Audiences (Toby)

The album was released in February 2017 via Ivy League/Mushroom records – a large independent label who normally release rock and pop music – and received media interest and reviews in various national and international outlets, including a 4.5-star review in *Rolling Stone* (Young 2017). The majority of the coverage noted the diversity of the musicians and performance styles featured on the record. The *Guardian* noted that it 'reflects the diversity of the Bankstown community' (Smith 2017). ABC radio's The Music Show featured a live performance from the band and an in-depth interview with the musicians about their various instruments and performance styles.[13] The album received airplay nationally across ABC radio and community radio, and one song, 'Minto Mall', was added to rotation on ABC's Double J.

The live iteration was programmed by leading Australian arts institutions with an international focus – Utp, Carriageworks, The National Gallery of Victoria, and Casula Powerhouse – in addition to the Sydney Festival performance that had already occurred. The media interest and in particular the attention from institutional, government-funded programmers, was much higher than my previous album. Based on this reception it seems fair to conclude that there was a marked interest within English-speaking, middle-class cosmopolitan society for music that combined cultural traditions.

What is also notable, however, is that there was virtually no interest in the album from the ethnically specific media of Sydney (i.e. Arabic and Vietnamese print and radio). We speculate that this was due to several factors: all the songs were in English, the music used a fundamentally Western musical architecture, the Western rock networks of Ivy League/Mushroom, the label that released the album, and the venues we played. Ultimately, despite the inclusive approach to composing and arranging parts for the record, and the free rein the musicians had, the limits of the album's audiences speak to the fact this was a project initiated and driven by me, Toby. This, however, was different in the next project we will discuss.

7 Project 2: *Song Khúc Lượn Bay/Two Sounds Gliding* (2018–2023)[14]

Musicians

Đăng Lan	đàn bầu, đàn tranh, vocals
Toby Martin	guitar, vocals
Bree van Reyk	drums and percussion
Matthew Steffen	electric and double bass

---

[13] Toby Martin's street songs www.abc.net.au/radionational/programs/musicshow/toby-martin-northam-avenue/8473368, accessed 1 February 2023.

[14] This project was also known as TÌNH KHÚC TỪ QUÊ HƯƠNG/ Songs From Home for some of the concerts

Recording engineers
Bob Scott

Composers
Đăng Lan and Toby Martin, with other contributors.[15]

Outcomes
One album. Concert performances for Sydney Festival at Casula Powerhouse; Bankstown Arts Centre; Phuoc Hue Temple, Fairfield Showgrounds Tết celebrations; small venues in Sydney and surrounds.

Financing
Urban Theatre Projects (Utp) commissioned Lan and Toby for artistic development. They were both paid the same fee for one week's work. Subsequent songwriting and arrangement with the two of them was unpaid. Toby paid for the studio, the other musicians, and the engineer Bob Scott through a combination of personal funding and an internal research grant from the University of Sydney.

Lan paid for an extra recording of one of the songs with engineer Phi Le using her own finances. For the Sydney Festival show at Casula Powerhouse all musicians were paid the same fee. The other performances were community fundraising events or were a door deal, evenly split.

Songwriting royalties are split according to the writers.

Writing/Background (Toby and Lan)

Songs from Northam Avenue was a project where the songs were written before collaboration occurred, different performance styles were juxtaposed and contrasted with each other – with the stiches showing – and the audience was almost entirely native English-speaking with a pre-existing interest in indie/pop/folk. *Song Khúc Lượn Bay/Two Sounds Gliding* was a deliberate response to the limitations of the previous project. It featured songs written in collaboration between us, it was an attempt to more seamlessly meld together Vietnamese and Western elements in order to find a 'new way', and it sought, and found, Vietnamese-speaking audiences and culturally Vietnamese performance

---

[15] Full composition credits: 1. 'Lý Cây Đa' ('Ballad of the Banyan Tree') Trad. English translation by Phạm Duy and Đăng Lan 'English Bridge' by Toby Martin. 2. 'God's Will' by Đăng Lan and Toby Martin. 3. 'Qua cầu gió bay' ('The Wind on the Bridge') Trad. English translation by Phạm Duy. 4. 'Tôi Là Ai' ('Who Am I?') – by Đăng Lan and Toby Martin. 5. 'When We Two Parted', poem by Lord Byron, translation into Vietnamese by Dương Quang Duy, music by Đăng Lan. 6. 'Cò Lả' ('The Stork') Trad. English translation by Đăng Lan. 7. 'Đôi Dép' ('Two Shoes') poem by Nguyễn Trung Kiên, music by Đăng Lan and Toby Martin. 8. 'Flowers in Hand' by Đăng Lan.

venues. It has been performed at a variety of venues in Sydney and western Sydney, and the album was released via ABC Music in February 2024.[16]

Like *Songs from Northam Avenue*, *Two Sounds Gliding* began as a commissioned residency with Utp. However, this time we were both equally employed as commissioned artists. The residency took place both in the rehearsal studios of Bankstown Arts Centre during an intensive one-week period in 2018, and then was followed up at Lan's house nearby on a semi-regular basis from 2019 (although interrupted by Covid-19). Two different types of song emerged from this period: original songs written by us, and re-imaginings of traditional Vietnamese material.

With regards to the original songs, the lyrics to these emerged from long conversations between us. These conversations were recorded and then useful sections or phrases extracted, shaped to have rhythm (and sometimes rhyme), and set to music. This technique intentionally captured the natural patterns of speech in order to give the songs a sense of veracity and to find lyrics that were fresh and not predictable. This approach has some ties to 'verbatim' theatre and to 'documentary' songwriting.[17] Because many of the lyrics do not sound like standard pop songwriting, they have a certain awkwardness on first listen but, we hope, they also have a freshness.[18]

This style of songwriting is particularly fruitful in situations where all participants are not experienced songwriters. Lan is a hugely knowledgeable singer, and masterful interpreter of songs by others, but had not had much experience in writing her own lyrics from scratch. This process helped to demystify the lyric-writing process, making it less intimidating and more easily accommodating of individual experience and word choice.

Conversations between us focussed on home and family. Lan in particular spoke a lot about her experiences of coming to Australia as a refugee in 1975: the terrifying departure from Saigon, the traumatic boat journey to Hong Kong, the first few months in Australia living in the East Hills Migrant Hostel, and the sense of eeriness that she felt in response to the new landscape: 'all around me/

---

[16] While the album is called *Song Khúc Lượn Bay/ Two Sounds Gliding*, this project has also been called *Tình Khúc Từ Quê Hương / Songs from Home*, and indeed was called so at its premiere performance for Sydney Festival at Casula Powerhouse in 2021.

[17] On verbatim theatre, see Summerskill 2020; also see 'Documentary Songwriters' www.docsong.org/, accessed 2 February 2023.

[18] This process of basing lyrics on conversation, or testimony, was used by Gomeroi elder Uncle Roger Knox, Jason Walker, and Toby during a previous songwriting residency at Campbelltown Arts Centre in 2013. Uncle Roger referred to our conversations as 'yarning' (a common descriptor amongst Indigenous people). The results of these yarns are a forthcoming album by Knox, and an already performed song, 'Black Tear Tracks', https://rogerknoxmusic.com/watch/media/black-tear-tracks/, accessed 29 December 2022.

only bush/ I feel so lonely' go the lyrics of 'Tôi là Ai'/ 'Who Am I?', the song we wrote about this experience. Lan also spoke about the ongoing sense of dislocation that comes with being a refugee, never feeling entirely at home in either country. The lyrics of 'Tôi là Ai' contrast her puzzlement about Australian customs – 'In Australia you have to ring first/ in Vietnam you just come around' – with her sense of estrangement she feels from the country of her birth – 'When I go back to Vietnam it doesn't feel the same/ I wonder has it changed?/ Or have I changed?'

'Tôi là Ai' is a good example of the ways in which songwriting can move between the specific and the general. Lan's story and lyrics are highly personal, but they resonated strongly with her community, the Vietnamese diaspora in Sydney:

> Yes that is their thought, that is their viewpoint. The song 'Tôi là Ai' captures that. Many of my Vietnamese friends here talk to me and tell me they have the same feeling that I have when I go back to Vietnam. When I have the time to chat with them, they say 'that's right, that's me', I feel the same . . . that is very common.

'Tôi là Ai'/ 'Who Am I?' is a sentiment that is also applicable to other communities that have experienced sudden and unwanted displacement across the world. But it also connects to something that many non-Indigenous people feel living in a settler-colonial society that we are not *from* anywhere, neither the place we live nor the place of our ancestors and the desire to create and explain a sense of 'belonging' (Read 2000). Vietnamese/Australian writer Sheila Pham describes living in western Sydney:

> Nowadays I prefer to say I live *on* Dharug land. After all, I wasn't born on this country, and ultimately 'on' seems more correct than 'from', a preposition which suggests a belonging I don't necessarily feel nor am especially entitled to . . .
> [western Sydney is] a place where many of us have put down our tentative roots. The area exists now because it existed before, and it existed long before that – and the ultimate truth is that most of us have no place else, realistically, to go. (Pham 2022. Emphasis in original)

'Tôi là Ai' is an example of the ways in which pop songwriting can wrestle productively with clichés. Questions of identity, belonging, and home are familiar, even staple, subjects of pop songwriting, yet this cliché is given fresh power and perspective, and twisted into new shapes, via Lan's story, the specifics of which are not heard often in pop songs.

Lan was also very responsive to ongoing global events, which she connected to her own personal experience of war. This provided the context to the lyrics of the song 'Flowers in Hand'. Unlike the other original songs, which were written together, this was written alone by Lan.

'Flowers in Hand' I wrote, because I have seen lots of war, and I grew up in the time of war, and also now at the time being, Ukraine, Russia, World War, wars bringing suffering to people … I feel so so so sad, I feel unhappy because of that, because of killing, because of suffering. The whole world now is very dangerous, and everywhere there is death and sickness and disaster, everything, and it strongly comes to my mind. And that's why I have the flowers in hand. I wrote 'Flowers in Hand' because of that.

I wrote the song because I was thinking about war but also thinking about the war in Vietnam. I am always thinking of that. And I suppose I want to write a song of war. I see so many deaths that sometimes I can't eat. This time I didn't eat much … all day I eat only one bowl. Because my husband listens to the radio and watches TV and sees so many deaths and it influences my mind and so sometimes I clean the bowls, I clean up, when I am cleaning, and I just talk, I talk to God. I say, 'God please stop the war, stop death.' I am always thinking of others' suffering. So it makes me … I really want to have happiness for the whole world.

Songwriting provided a nourishing and poetic way to work through this sadness and to produce something of beauty from it. The writing process of this song was that Lan went to the bathroom and came back some fifteen minutes later with the lyrics fully written out in her head. She described the process thus:

I don't know why it suddenly came into my mind … on that day I read the newspaper, and I saw so many deaths. I washed my hands, and then I thought of my hands now. Pure. And clean. And I want to hold something nice and beautiful. Something nice and clear. Inside. Pure, purify. I want to purify my mind. That's why I wrote it.

The lyrics are written like a chant:

Flowers in hands I pray to my god/ Flowers in hand I pray to Buddha
Flowers in hand I pray to Jesus/ Flowers in hand I pray to Allah
Flowers in hand I pray for the whole world/ No more war, we'll have happiness
No more war, not having suffering

There was a cultural difference around the idea of songwriting for us. Songwriting is often about walking the line between autobiography and fiction, and about presenting a persona to an audience that is neither entirely true nor entirely fake. It is often confessional, or assumed to be confessional. This style of songwriting was natural for me, but confronting for Lan – it made her feel exposed and also she was worried that her friends would think she was putting herself on a pedestal by singing about herself. This was particularly the case with the song 'God's Will' which is about her son:

I don't say I am humble. I don't want to say that. But sometimes I feel shy. When people pay so much attention to me. Like when I go out. Even when I go out with my friends, my girlfriends, I want them to be the same, the same like me. If I wear nice clothes and they don't wear nice clothes I don't feel good. Because I don't want to be a princess, or act so important. So when we write about my story, about my family, my son, I have both feelings. One: I feel so shy. I want to be in a quiet place. I don't want people to know me so much. And then I feel . . . why not!?

My experiences were also the subject of conversation and songwriting. The song 'Pure Land' (which we never made a studio recording of, and so is not on the album) combined the Buddhist phrase for enlightenment with ideas of looking for a land of belonging (Tâm 1991). I began this project with Lan while living in northern England, a place that my maternal grandfather was *from* and in some ways I felt connected to, but also felt distant from. The idea of a 'pure land' becomes a place where one feels at home, but as the song discusses, this is a place searched for, rather than found. And is a state of mind, as much as a geographic region. This song contrasts my experience of trying to find identity in England – 'So I move to England/ Where people grow like mushrooms/ At night the lights stretch out/ I wonder where I'll find room' – with Lan's feeling of estrangement and guilt: 'If I forget Vietnam/ Am I guilty, am I disloyal?/ I wake up I can't remember/ My motherland at all' and then in the chorus we combine our thoughts: 'Where do I belong?/ Where do I belong?/ For better or worse, right or wrong/ I'm looking for my pure land'.

Another song 'Cat and Pig' which was not recorded for the final album contrasts our vastly different life experiences. While I was born into Anglo, middle-class comfort in 1975 in Melbourne, Lan migrated to Australia as a refugee in 1975.The lyrics go: 'In the winter of 1975/ Into a cold country you arrived/ In the same place, the same year I was born/ Given a name, given a passport that was my own'. Despite these differences, we were able to find common ground to work together over an extended period of time and become close friends. This song is a reflection on our differences but also our compatibility. The song title 'Cat and Pig' comes from the year of our births according to the Vietnamese lunar calendar. I was born in the year of the cat, Lan in the year of the pig, and this, according to Lan's Buddhist philosophy, makes us compatible despite the extreme differences in our life experiences: 'When I work with someone else, we are mostly compatible because of the year we're born. And Toby is the year of cat and I am the year of pig. Our personalities are very important. We match.'

Arrangements (Toby and Lan)

With regards to the re-imaginings of the traditional Vietnamese songs, this came about through Lan teaching me many songs aurally. Some of the songs Lan translated into English for me to sing (like 'Lý Cây Đa'/ 'Ballad of the Banyan Tree'), other songs Lan taught me to sing in Vietnamese (like 'Cò Lả'/ 'The Stork'). This process of learning to sing the songs in Vietnamese was an important part of understanding how the musical material functioned. Singing in Vietnamese provided an embodied feeling of music and language. When I put my mouth around the words it gives me a better insight into the music somehow, it makes me understand how the music works. Because the language itself is reliant on pitch and phrasing.

The more Lan and I played the songs, the more they started to take on elements that marked them as different to the standard, or traditional, way of performing them. These elements were taken from my embodied performance practices. They included a Western style of singing that featured less pronounced pitch inflections and ornamentations than Vietnamese singing; parts sung in English; use of punk and post-punk guitar textures, including alternative tunings which provided different types of sonorities and overhanging notes, and use of excessively 'fuzzed out' distortion both on the guitar and the đàn bầu (seen in 'Qua Cầu Gió Bay'/ 'The Wind on the Bridge'); use of rock band instrumentation (guitar/bass/drums) combining with the Vietnamese instruments; and new sections, composed by Toby, inserted into old songs (for instance the bridge section in 'Lý Cây Đa'/ 'Ballad of the Banyan Tree').

For Lan, after having played this traditional style of music for some fifty years, these many changes and interventions in the song material represented a 'new way':

> the thing I like best is that Toby and I do these songs, my traditional songs, but we both sing in both languages and also Toby adds some of his own version. Australian style. I love that.
> ... that is the new way. Since I've been playing Vietnamese music, I have seen no one do it before ... This is the first time we do that in this way ... We have combined Western and Eastern styles.

While Lan uses the term 'Australian' style, I prefer the term 'Western style'. This difference in terminology indicates the different ways in which we see our national cultures and the different ideas about cultural inclusivity.

T: I was going to ask you … the music we make … do you think that is Australian music?

L: Not quite Australian music, but not quite Vietnamese either. I mean, mixed. It's different.

T: But why can't it be Australian music? Like maybe it's just new Australian music?

L: We can say it's combined music.

The combination of sounds – 'Western' and 'Eastern', 'Australian' and 'Vietnamese' – not only merged together, but also produced interesting aesthetic juxtapositions. For instance, the lyrics in Flowers in Hand are about cross-cultural understanding, and yet the unrelenting drone behind it emphasises the bleakness and sadness of the song's context. Similarly, 'Qua Cầu Gió Bay'/ 'The Wind on the Bridge' is a widely known and loved song in Vietnam. Its lyrics are from the point of a view of a young woman who is meeting her lover clandestinely. She is telling her lover that when she returns home she will lie to her parents, telling them that the reason she is missing her ring and hat is because the wind on the bridge has blown them away (not because she has given them to her lover!). This is widely thought of as a very romantic song in Vietnam and is invariably performed in a slow tempo, with a soft, lyrical quality. For our version, though, we underlined the darker elements of the song (secrecy and lying) with a much more taut and unresolved arrangement that emphasises tension and drama.

However, sometimes such juxtapositions changed the meaning too much. For instance, while Lan approved of the new arrangement of 'Qua Cầu Gió Bay'/ 'Wind on the Bridge', she objected to the proposed imagery set to the music. For the show at Casula Powerhouse we commissioned artist Lyndal Irons to take photos and videos of us to project behind us as we played. One of the films was of us doing a stylised sword display. Lan is a kung fu and tai chi practitioner and teacher, and had taught me some moves. When Lyndal set 'Qua Cầu Gió Bay'/ 'The Wind on the Bridge' to this film, Lan was adamantly against it because of the way in which it contradicted the romantic meaning of the song: 'Kung fu is about fighting, but that song is not about fighting. It has a lovely meaning. The kung fu film is just concerned with my background and activities; it is not concerned with the meaning of the song.'

I argued that that was the point, the juxtaposition of image and lyrical material was deliberate and artistic; but Lan vetoed the idea. Instead she chose a much more lyrical video of banana trees swaying in the breeze: 'Because the wind on the bridge is a very floating song, floating and soft. The meaning of the song is very romantic and soft. So I liked something windy, like the breeze.'

Ultimately, this argument was very fruitful as it exposed some fundamental differences between our approaches to art making. It revealed the tensions between modernist ideas of deliberately contrasting elements, on the one hand, with Vietnamese traditional art practices which valued continuity, and novelty with limitations, on the other. This project was in some ways a constant negotiation of these aesthetic and moral ideas. Most commonly these were negotiated via the music making itself and finding a middle ground that both parties were happy with. The argument about 'The Wind on the Bridge' was one of the very few times that we couldn't agree, and in this case was resolved by acceding to Lan's authority as cultural knowledge-holder. Referring back to Bowman's (2016) framework of 'virtue ethics', arguments and differences are important, especially in cross-cultural settings. They indicate that the relationships are robust, rather than acquiescent, and not ones where people simply say 'yes' for convenience or to avoid conflict.

Recording (Lan and Toby)

The recording of the songs also showed how differences in approaches could be resolved, sometimes by doing two different versions of the same song. The album recordings were organised by me, recorded live with the four-piece rock band, with engineer Bob Scott, while Lan organised the extra recording with Phi Le with digitally created backing tracks.

The use of a live rock band versus backing tracks is also one that is culturally dependent. While I am from a Western rock tradition of using live instrumentation, Lan preferred programmed drums, synth pads, and synthesised strings. I also preferred a rawer, tense style, while Lan preferred a more romantic/sentimental style popular with the south Vietnamese diaspora (Norton 2009: 27). This is not simply a different process, it created very different aesthetic outcomes. The 'Toby' approach is rougher and has less consistency of pitch and a greater emphasis on energy and dynamics; the 'Lan' approach is often more consistent both in tempo and pitch and overall has a smoother, glossier, quality. These two approaches can be seen in the recorded version of 'When We Two Parted'. For this song, Lan took the lyrics of the well-known Lord Byron poem, translated into Vietnamese by Quang Duy, and set them to music. We sang it as a romantic duet, in Vietnamese and English respectively. The 'Toby' recording of the song, engineered by Bob Scott, is ultra stripped back, with just a lightly strummed acoustic guitar for accompaniment, and goes for four minutes. The 'Lan' version of the song, engineered by Phi Le, goes for fifteen minutes. It has a lush synth string accompaniment, programmed drums, and also features an extended spoken-word monologue.[19] This monologue is referred to as a 'recitation' and is an important tradition in Vietnamese popular music, and Lan is a highly experienced reciter.

> I thought the version we did with Bob was ok, but I wanted to include more musical parts for inspiration. I thought if we had more music, like cello, or violin, I would much prefer it. The end result to me sounds more touching. I think the sound is better. It makes people listen and have more feelings. It is also more appropriate to the song. Just guitar and singing is a more modern style. And the poem was written in the nineteenth century, it is from a classical time. Cello and violin and recitation suits the time it was written.

It is also notable that while Byron's poem is part of the canon of English language poetry, the decision to use it very much came from Lan, drawing on the prominence of romantic poetry in Vietnamese popular culture, and the tradition of the 'recitation'.

The music composed, arranged, and recorded in this project – both the original songs and the re-arrangements – represented an attempt to find a place where indie-folk-rock and Vietnamese popular traditions could meet, mingle, and emerge as something new. This new way had a clear aesthetic purpose, but it also had a moral/political dimension. In fact, the aesthetic and the moral dimensions are almost impossible to separate. The 'new way' was not just a musical direction, but also a new way in which to give voice to both artistic partners equally. In a landscape such as Australia, with entrenched power hierarchies and imbalances, this seemed pressing and important.

Decisions, Respect, Karma, and Time (Toby and Lan)

Questions about which studio to use, or how much distortion to put on an instrument, or what image should accompany a song were indicative of bigger questions about respect, compatibility, and relationships. Such questions are nuanced, and both of us have slightly different interpretations of how they might be answered, with Lan's approach very much influenced by Buddhism, for instance. We share here some of our conversation to capture the ways in which we have different ways of conceptualising the project.

T: What do you think about how we made decisions? How we decide. Do you think there has been a leader? Or do you think it has been a democracy?

---

[19] Compare www.youtube.com/watch?v=zT7Dfhk5R3o with www.youtube.com/watch?v=yCrHf8OShbQ.

L: No. I like to be free . . . I don't like to be a leader.

T: But in the things we've done together . . . how would you describe that? Democracy? Dictatorship?

L: No, no, I don't think it's a dictatorship. Ah I think you and me are compatible. So that's why I was able to work with you these last years. And if I felt dictated to, I would quit! So we work together well, we feel free, easy, relaxed. I don't feel pressure.

T: So compatible is a good word. Can you describe what you mean when you say that? So how are we compatible?

L: I believe that when I work with someone else, mostly we are compatible because of the year we are born. And you are the year of the cat and I am the year of the pig. You know our personality is very important. We match.

T: Ok, I like that. But let's imagine that there is another Đăng Lan and another Toby Martin here, and they are thinking of working together: what would you say to them? What do they need to do? Like, what type of people do they need to be, to be able to work together?

L: They need to respect each other. Mostly in talent, in capacity. Because you have something you do very well, and in this way you are good, but in another way different. Me too. The same. So we have to understand each other. The most important thing is that we accept it. That we accept the things that are not suited to do with each other. And then we find out the way to combine things together. We find out the good way to be in harmony. But if we don't have different ideas, how can we find out the new way? So we have to accept, and have understanding, and find out the good way to work together.

T: I think that's a really beautiful way of putting it actually. I like that. Respect.

L: To respect your idea.

T: And to accept that things are different.

L: And then we find out the way. Work it out together. Because the music is very immense, no limit, so the more you go through music and the more you find out – something else, something else, you know, the more you want to know.

The issue of time spent together is important too – especially time spent together not making music but sharing meals, sharing stories, sharing lives, simply being friends. However, we have different ideas about how important this is and a different interpretation of events.

T: You know, MohammadReza, he said a really important thing in these types of projects is time, a long time, so because I first met you, I think it was in 2015 and now it's 2022, it's seven years, and that's a long time, and we've been meeting and making music throughout that time, so do you think that's important? When you are trying to make something new and different that you need a long time to do it?

L: No. When I first met you, the first time, I felt like I had met you somewhere before. Like I had met you a long time ago. Like I had been knowing you a long time. I believe that. That is karma. That is like a string to bind you and me working together. I don't think you came to me incidentally, no, it has to be because of something before in a previous life.

T: So you think that happens straight away?

L: The first I met you I felt like you were my relative or my friend or my close friend from a long long time ago. And after one week you came a second time and I had a feeling, I felt like, you and me can be together, can work together.

T: So, if you want to make it work, you have to have met in a previous life?

L: Maybe next time you will be my father . . . ? (haha hahah)

T: Maybe I was already! What about all the other things. Because after seven years . . . you cook lots of amazing meals, I eat at your house, you've been to my house a few times for dinner, I make not so amazing meals, we drive around Sydney, like we do things . . . we actually do a lot of things that are not making music. We probably spend more time doing things that are not music, than we do music, so for a good musical relationship, do you think it's important to have other relationships . . . sharing a meal . . .

L: Yeah, the music brings you happiness and makes you feel peaceful and relaxed. We meet together because of music and I think that the music brings us together. And then later, our personalities work, we are compatible.

T: So actually, you're saying, it's the other way around. You make music together, and that enables you to be friends.

L: So when I work with you I feel not pushed or stressed. I feel free. I feel relaxed. That's why I wrote the songs . . .

Interestingly, we both think that an easy-going and respectful relationship has been a central part of making music together. However, while Lan thinks that music creates an environment in which such a relationship can flourish, Toby tends to think that it is the time spent together doing non-musical things that positively influences the music. But clearly both aspects influence each other.

Audiences (Toby and Lan)

Unlike for *Songs from Northam Avenue*, audiences for this project have comprised both native English-speaking and native Vietnamese-speaking. In 2020 we performed as part of the Tet/Lunar New Year festival at Phuoc Hue Buddhist Temple, in western Sydney, for an audience almost exclusively from the Vietnamese-speaking diaspora. In 2021 we performed in front of mixed audiences at Casula Powerhouse, for the Sydney Festival, and at Bankstown Arts Centre for their twentieth anniversary. In 2024, for the launch of the album, we performed in small clubs in Sydney. For the Casula Powerhouse/ Sydney Festival show all promotional material – the physical flyer and the web site – as well as the program notes were written in Vietnamese and English.

Many of Lan's friends and extended community were at these shows, and Lan was very aware of what they thought. Lan's delight in the 'new way' was reflected in comments made to her by members of this community.

> My friends say they are so excited, and they say that it's new, they have never heard it before. They didn't know this way before, they only listen to Vietnamese traditional music … they like something new, to change. Just like when you eat. If you eat bread all the time, or you eat rice every day, you feel fed up. I want to have something else. Noodles? Or Italian food? Or Japanese food?

This reaction was also found in a younger Vietnamese/Australian audience who had grown up with the traditional Vietnamese music of their parents and with alternative rock of the late twentieth and early twenty-first centuries that they were hearing at the radio and at gigs. People who had grown up with both famous Vietnamese songwriters like Trịnh Công Sơn and Western indie bands like the Smiths. People like this we spoke to found the new versions we did novel and interesting.

Vietnamese audiences were also interested in my singing in Vietnamese. This mirrored a fascination with foreign singers coming to Vietnam and singing Vietnamese material, such as the American singer Kyo York.[20] The exoticism was commented on. As Lan said to me:

---

[20] https://vietnamnet.vn/en/a-foreign-voice-singing-local-songs-726048.html, accessed 8 March 2023.

> My friends liked your singing! They said it was very interesting. They said it was the first time they had seen an Australian man singing a Vietnamese folk song. They liked how you sang clearly Vietnamese in an Australian accent. They liked that. They thought it was lovely.

I was initially quite uncomfortable singing in Vietnamese. It seemed, from the outset, like an appropriation of a culture that I was not embedded in. To refer back to the literature in the introduction to this Element, my singing in Vietnamese seemed like an example of hooks' idea of 'spice', Hage's idea of 'white multi-culturalism' or Robinson's idea of 'extractivism'. However, for Lan, this was the aspect of the project that she was most excited and energised by. She enjoyed teaching me the Vietnamese lyrics, hearing me perform them, and showing this to her community. For her, this was a novel and exotic phenomena. This became a source of much of the pleasure Lan took in the project, and, as outlined in the introduction, locating where musicians derive pleasure is an important factor in projects such as these. Importantly, it was also one of the things that transferred cultural authority to her and placed me in a more vulnerable situation. This helped to erode hierarchies in a project where I often asked Lan to step outside of her comfort zone. I could now reciprocate by stepping outside of my comfort zone.

Western audiences commented more on the original songs, partly because they were predominantly in English, but also because they gave personal accounts of bigger social issues which were not as familiar to non-Vietnamese audiences. In this, these songs constituted a personal way of telling bigger historical stories.

> A few of my friends – Australian friends, not Vietnamese friends – said they went to see our performance. They liked the original songs. Such as 'Tôi là Ai'. They liked the way that the song is a story, it is historical music, that is something different.
>
> Performing at Phuoc Hue Buddhist Temple, compared to performing at Casula Powerhouse. It's a different atmosphere. In front of our community, at our community functions, because they have eating, and talking, and so they can't concentrate on what you do on stage, so I have to sing in a different way, a different style of music. But with Australian audiences, they give more of their attention, watching, they give their whole mind, to watch and enjoy it.
>
> When you play đàn bầu and đàn tranh, it needs a very quiet atmosphere, and Australian audiences, whatever they listen to, they always keep their mind on the music and the song.
>
> So I feel I can share my feelings with them more easily. But in the Vietnamese style, with a Vietnamese audience, well it depends on the venue. If you sing for a party it's different to the concert. If it's a concert it's very good. They keep quiet because there is no eating, no talking, they concentrate their mind onto the stage.

The album was released by ABC Music in 2024, just at the time of finishing writing this book, and so we do not yet have a lot of data on the reaction of audiences to the recording. However, ABC pursued opportunities to market the album to English and Vietnamese speaking people, and as well as a digital release, we manufactured CDs specifically because Lan thought these would be more desirable than streaming for people in her community.

The different audiences, their different expectations, and their different behaviours were indicative of the way this project attempted to bridge two worlds, Lan's and mine. We asked each other to do new and different things – for Lan that might have been to write a confessional song, for me that might have been to sing in Vietnamese. We tried different arrangement ideas, and different production ideas, both Lan's preference and mine. We felt a karmic connection and a strong sense of trust, which enabled us to voice fairly strong differences of opinion. Of all the three projects, this one represented the most equitable distribution of decision making, and best captured an attempt to love across difference.

8 Project 3: *I Felt the Valley Lifting* (2018–2022)

Players

Seyed MohammadReza Beladi	Ney, neyanban, dammam
George Harrington	Drums
Toby Martin	Guitar, vocals
Julia Morgan	Tin whistle, flute
Chris Ruffoni	Electric bass, trumpet
Sarah Tym	Northumbrian smallpipes, violin

Engineer

Colin Elliot

Composer

Toby Martin

Outcomes

One Album. Two concerts in Huddersfield and York, and one performance at Onwards Festival, Huddersfield

Funding

Toby paid the musicians for rehearsals and recordings from his own finances. This was a flat fee that equated to approximately one week's full-time work. The engineer and studio were paid by an internal research grant from the University of Huddersfield. The two concerts were a door deal and the money was split between the musicians. Onwards Festival paid a flat fee which was also split equally between the musicians.

Songwriting and Background (Toby)

Unlike the first two case studies, the third project did not take place in western Sydney, but in west Yorkshire. I lived in a small village, called Slaithwaite, outside Huddersfield, UK, in Kirklees council from 2015 to 2019. During my last year there I wrote a suite of songs about life in the village. Like *Songs from Northam Avenue* these songs were inspired by the people and stories of a particular place. In this case those people were my friends and neighbours, rather than residency 'hosts', and the place was a post-industrial, pre-Brexit village, rather than a metropolitan suburb. The songs that I wrote were story songs, and as such fit within the narrative, ballad tradition of British Isles folk songs. However, rather than being about fishing or coal mining, or other traditional subject matter of northern English folk, these songs were about contemporary concerns: neighbours sharing wi-fi, the underlying racist violence of Brexit, sudden moments of natural beauty, school appeals.

The melodies for these songs were also folk-like. They were based on modal forms, had a relatively large pitch movement, and were elongated with the melody often stretching over six bars or more, in comparison to the shorter, repeated melodic material of my previous rock songs with their usually fairly small pitch range. The songs were also based around very limited harmonic movement, often a drone, or at least only one or two chord changes. This sense of a drone was emphasised through my guitar tuning in which the bottom strings were a series of fourths (the guitar was tuned to D/G/D/G/B/E). The modal melodies could thus emerge from the drone, implying major and minor movement without necessarily resolving into either.

Like *Songs from Northam Avenue*, once the basic outlines of the songs were written, I invited musicians from the local area to arrange parts for the songs. These musicians played a variety of styles – British Isles folk music, Persian classical and folk, rock, and brass band music – and thus represented some of the diversity of music making in and around Huddersfield. This cultural diversity was a strong aspect of life in West Yorkshire, but not one that was apparent from the outside, or at least was not communicated very well. I remember arriving in Huddersfield and being blown away by the variety of cultures and music making that was going on – reggae, bhangra, Kurdish music, Persian music. The popular image of Yorkshire is rural and white, rather like the box for 'Yorkshire Tea' which shows green fields, sheep, cricket players and stone walls. It is supposed to sum up Yorkshire. But what is in the box is far more diverse and far more interesting than what the box suggests.

The Huddersfield area has attracted waves of migrants in the twentieth century due to its concentration of industry, in particular textile factories, itself the result of Huddersfield's rapid development during the Industrial Revolution. People have come from the Caribbean and South Asia, and more recently central Asia and Africa, with Kurdish, Iranian, and Somali refugees being a significant minority in the last few decades. Migrants brought their musical cultures with them, which adapted and changed to the conditions of northern England. Huddersfield has been a particular centre for reggae and soundsystem culture and for bhangra (Huxtable 2014; Sahota 2014).[21]

As mentioned in the prologue to the Element, MohammadReza and I met at his sandwich shop in 2017. We got talking, and then jamming, and one thing led to another. I asked him to work with me facilitating songwriting and music workshops at a drop-in centre for refugees in Huddersfield. We taught students together, and I supervised his Master's thesis. Beladi now is a much more appreciated and recognisable part of the Huddersfield musical landscape, and performed as part of the Kirklees Year of Music 2023 celebrations, has worked with students at the University and has recently graduated with a PhD.

Arrangements: Technical Concerns (Toby and MohammadReza)

In a similar fashion to the Northam Avenue project, players were asked to write their own parts in improvised group settings. MohammadReza and I had some preliminary one-on-one sessions in order to get our heads around what each other's instruments did and how things would blend. These sessions were not aimed exclusively at *I Felt the Valley Lifting* but were part of a more general sharing of music that had some one-off performance and workshop outcomes. I also rehearsed separately with George on (drums) and Chris (bass) where we fleshed out the rhythmic and dynamic feel of the songs as a 'rock trio'. Chris also worked on some important arrangement ideas and wrote the brass parts. Nevertheless, the majority of the arrangement work happened in rehearsal studios with everyone present, or in the studio itself during overdubs.

This project had a noisier, wilder, more punk aesthetic than the previous two projects, due to the songs, the concept, playing styles, and the rehearsal environment. The rooms were small and the band was loud, and musicians had to create parts that would either contribute to the wall of sound or rise above it at key moments. Consequently, for the two bagpipe players, MohammadReza and Sarah Tym, there were extended sections where they stayed on one or two droning notes as accompaniment to the song, and others where they provided a lyrical, or strident, lead line (see 'Dark Red Blood' and 'Bird Boy' for examples of both approaches in the same song).

---

[21] The Town Sounds website and podcast is an excellent place to explore Huddersfield's rich history of music making: https://townsounds.co.uk/, accessed 30 December 2022.

As MohammadReza describes, the musicians found their way into composing individual parts by combining existing performance styles with improvisation.

> Most of the pieces I played in these works were improvised at the beginning, but gradually these improvised pieces gained a necessary maturity and kept their place as fixed components in the song. With the passing of time and the clarification of the musical structure, I was able to be creative in the performance and play the pieces more smoothly.

Like Lan, MohammadReza also grappled with the technical challenges of playing in unfamiliar keys. Just as Lan had to get a different string for the đàn bầu, MohammadReza had to make adaptations to his instruments:

> 'For better coordination in the performance of the pieces, I ordered a new neyanban chanter whose tuning was suitable for the song "Strange Fish" for example, and these qualitative improvements in my work were achieved over time.'

While the marriage of Persian instruments and performance styles with rock and British Isles folk is not a common one, and presented plenty of technical challenges, there were some common features across the styles that surprised and encouraged us. The strongest one was the reliance on drones and a minimal sense of harmonic movement. A second, but related one, was the use of modal melodies. Sometimes in Persian music these are set patterns which can be transferred to new contexts. In Arabic music, which the music of Bushehr draws on to some extent, these patterns are called 'maqams' and have been applied in Persian classical or art music as dastgāh (Farraj and Shumays 2019). The idea of a drone, with a lilting melody on top of it, became a unifying feature of this project. Another commonality was the sense of rawness. Imperfect pitch, irregular tempos, the valuing of expressivity over virtuosity – these are important qualities of traditional vernacular musics of both Bushehr and northern England (and punk, for that matter). These stylistic similarities provided an important aesthetic template.

The punk aesthetic of not being technically perfect, but valuing feel, experimentation, and creativity also extended across this project. All of us were slightly out of our comfort zones to some extent, playing with instruments we had never played with before, or in styles that were unnatural. We were coming unstuck from our usual working methods. For MohammadReza, while he was very fluent as a percussionist, he was far less comfortable with wind instruments.

> The truth is that I am the composer and director in my group, but I use other musicians to perform the works, and I usually only sing or play dammam. In other words, before working with this band, I was familiar with instruments like neyanban or ney, but I had never officially played with these instruments on stage, so also in this respect, it was a new experience and challenge for me.

Our practice-based observations about the similarities between Persian and Northern English vernacular forms were reflected in archival historical and musicological research. In the *Origins of the Popular Style*, Peter van de Merwe writes that musical civilisation came from the Near East (i.e. modern-day Arabic and Persian countries) some 4,000 years ago. Pre-Islamic and Islamic culture spread into Europe, reaching its peak influence in the 1300s. While its influence then declined in metropolitan western Europe, its style remained on 'the edges':

> The countryside ... inaccessible places like islands and mountains, and the eastern and northern extremities of Europe were longest to cling to the old ways .... This explains why so much that is Oriental in character lingered on in the folk music of Scotland and Ireland ... Situated in the north-western corner of Europe, they kept up folk styles that had once been current over the whole continent. (van de Merwe 1992: 13)

MohammadReza's own research has also shown how recognisable, even iconic, musical features of the northern and western extremities of the British Isles had Persian and Arabic origins. For instance, the neyanban and similar bagpipes found in modern-day Egypt, were taken by Roman soldiers to the northern parts of Britain, and adopted and adapted by the Scots, Irish and Northumbrians. Ref: The bagpipe famously relies on drones for its powerful and haunting sound – and the number of possible drones has increased with technological advancements – with the chanter providing the melodic variations. MohammadReza and Sarah Tym's bagpipes had very different qualities: the neyanban is much louder and the pitch more unregulated than the quieter, more lyrical Northumbrian smallpipes, and yet their similarities are also striking and aesthetically interesting. The songs on this project effectively had a 'double drone' from two separate bagpipes. These drones were not just different in pitch, but also different in texture. In some ways the guitar too with its doubling of open fourths was a third drone element.

Arrangements: Conceptual Concerns, Leadership, and Democracy (Toby and MohammadReza)

> The combination of different cultures that are considered unknown to each other may seem strange and difficult at first, but over time they find their way to dialogue and become the basis for the birth of another culture .... the fusion of elements of other cultures in another is the basis for a cultural amalgamation, which in turn contributes to the development and enrichment of cultures.
>
> The same thing has been happening for years in multicultural societies like Bushehr whose music I depict in this work, and whose music is the result of the interaction and fusion of different cultures.
>
> Practically, the same thing happened in this group, that is, many of the members and their music were unknown to each other, but with the provision of the

necessary platform and the passage of time, the sounds became familiar and a dialogue started between them.

MohammadReza's statement that he is depicting the music of Bushehr resonates with a central idea across the three projects, namely that existing performance practices are brought in and recontextualised.

> As a musician from the south of Iran, with the Valley Lifting group I have brought the instruments and cultural elements of my small geographical region into a different cultural context. The music of Bushehr itself has developed in a multicultural context, but what distinguishes this music and its instruments, in general, is a combination of the unique timbres, the patterns of musical tones, the rhythms, and generally the different accents and musical expression. The use of each of these features, which represent the particular cultural elements, individually or in combination in a different musical genre, such as pop music, creates a new musical expression. Within the existing structure of the songs that were given to me, and the limitations of my musical instruments, I tried to use some of these features of Bushehr's music in my parts.

One key concern for MohammadReza was how to compose parts for songs that had already been written, yet also stay true to his established performance practice and language. MohammadReza vividly describes this tension, but also the opportunities it presented, as the invitation for him to come up with parts was a slightly new way of working:

> I and some of the other musicians were invited to a house that was already set up and we had to find a place for ourselves. This was an open and democratic platform for musical work to crystallise and flourish. I asked Toby about the specific role he expected me to play in each of the songs, and Toby gave a brief explanation. It seemed he wanted to see how I could write the best role for myself.
>
> Well, these were things that sometimes reminded me of my own approach in my group Leymer, and sometimes deviated from what I had practiced in my group before. Indeed, I too count on the expertise of each person in Leymer, and I expect their particular artistic skills to be effective in creating the nuances of the work, but I define each person's role in advance. The role of the neyanban in our music group is a little different because this instrument is usually open to improvisation due to its traditional position and nature. I always give my friends the saying that the director's thoughts come from your tongue with your expression. But during the preparation of the songs, I listen to the suggestions and use their opinion to edit the work.

Time (Toby and MohammadReza)

For more than thirty years I have been performing on stage with the musical instruments of Bushehr in the form of the Leymer group, a folk music group from Bushehr, but the experience of working with this (Valley Lifting) group was quite different. During my artistic career there were several times I worked with groups representing other musical cultures and each had its own characteristics. An important aspect of this project was that nobody dictated anything. But rather, it was left to the various cultural elements collected to find their own way in the riverbed of this music.

The recent experience with this group was a different and valuable experience due to the relatively long duration of this collaboration. During this period there was enough time to develop and mature the thoughts that had arisen in me as a musician about the way of working together and the philosophy of the work, for Toby as the songwriter and for the other members of the group to work together in the best possible way. At the beginning of this collaboration, everything was very vague and unclear to me, and I needed time to find my way as part of this group. Understanding what is expected of me, what I am supposed to do, and what I can do, especially with the kind of musical instruments I have and my own personal capability, took time.

For MohammaReza, the openness of collaboration and the perceived lack of direction created some lack of clarity at first, but ultimately paid off as it gave him the freedom to experiment and find his own way in the group. The success of this is due not just to the philosophy of openness, but also to the experience of the musicians. MohammadReza also points out that a musical connection occurs as a result of a personal connection, and intercultural relationships:

> The fusion of cultures actually started in rehearsals, not from a musical point of view, but as an association of people from different cultural backgrounds who came together to interact with each other and hoped that this interaction would bring good results. Collaboration brings connection. But this means that we have to build our own relationships first so that a musical work or anything else can emerge from these good relationships. And finally, after that joint creation, these relationships reach a level that can be relied upon.

Đăng Lan had a different interpretation of how to sequence events – stressing the importance of a karmic connection before the collaboration began, while MohammadReza and I thought that time spent developing the relationships spurred the connection. In either case, we considered the length of time, and personal/social connections as vital to the projects, even if we explained how it was vital in different ways different ways.

Individual Songs (MohammadReza)

Given the complexity of MohammadReza's musical culture and the nuances of approach he took to the arrangements for each song, it would be useful at this point to look at what he brought to individual songs in some detail.

'Town Gossip'
The song 'Town Gossip' was a song in which I played ney and dammam. This song was one in which I tried to incorporate as strongly as possible musical

features of Bushehr and Iranian music into my performance. I have high-lighted the word 'Iranian music' next to 'Bushehr' because the style I have chosen for playing the ney in this work is the method and style used in classical Iranian music for this instrument, and it is called Ney-e Haft Band. This style is different from the style normally used in ethnic-based folk music. In this song, I have used one of the special scales of Bushehr music, namely the song of Sharveh, in addition to the different tone colour of the ney, which is considered a novel sound in pop music. As mentioned earlier, the musical pieces I performed with the ney in this work were all improvised, but the use of Bushehr's musical tone patterns in this work, and especially the use of microtones, gave this work a different musical expression.

The instrument dammam is a percussion instrument that I played in the last section of this song. The dammam was used here not only as a percussion instrument, but also as a folk instrument of Bushehr, which brings a strong cultural flavour to this song. These characteristics include a certain accent that is traditionally followed when playing the rhythm with this instrument. In other words, I have tried to use the dammam instrument not only as a percussion instrument but for its folk flavour. Another point that can be mentioned about the performance of the dammam in this song is the style and figure of my playing with the dammam during the concerts. I have tried to make my playing posture physically like that of a local musician playing the dammam at a folk ritual in Bushehr.[22]

'Strange Fish'

'Strange Fish' was one of the songs on which I played the neyanban. The part I played in this song was a version of the main melody line of the song. After I prepared a new chanter for my neyanban, it became more satisfying than before because the key of the new chanter was closer to that song. I felt that the timbre of the neyanban suited this song very well because it gives the work the feel of a folk song, especially alongside another bagpipe from the north-east of England played by Sarah Tym, the Northumbrian Bagpipe. The idea of using two different types of bagpipes, one from Iran and one from Britain, together in this collection was one of the interesting ideas on this record.

'Dark Red Blood'

In the song 'Dark Red Blood', I also played neyanban, but it was different from 'Strange Fish'. In this song, my instrument represented exactly a Bushehri and Iranian neyanban. I played the same non-metric piece, called 'Hajiuni', which is played in Bushehr. The piece was a response to Toby's guitar part and showcased a different way of playing within a rock music format.

---

[22] See Macdonald (2021) 'I Felt The Valley Lifting' to see MohammadReza playing the dammam and neyanabn (www.youtube.com/watch?v=7w_OWeWgenE&t=407s at 5:50).

'The German Sea'

I added my part to 'The German Sea' after the studio recording and for subsequent concerts (and as such there is no recording of this). Initially, I was supposed to play the ney for this song, but despite my efforts, the result was not satisfactory, or at least did not satisfy my opinion. Perhaps it was because of the difference between the key of the song and my ney that I could not find common tones between the instrument and the song, so I gave up. But after the studio recording and for the concert we had in September 2022, I provided another ney whose key had the necessary coordination with that song, and I could accompany the band in concert. Finally, I played ney for the 'German Sea' song, although I played more improvised.

Recording (Toby)

We recorded the album in 2019 at Yellow Arch in Sheffield, with Colin Elliot engineering. Colin had worked mostly with indie rock acts such as Pulp, Jarvis Cocker, and Richard Hawley. Tracking was done partly live, but also with quite a few overdubs. Unlike *Songs from Northam Avenue*, all musicians were comfortable and experienced in overdubbing and preferred to spend some time on this process to develop their parts. Overdubs also provided a controlled situation where the quieter instruments, such as violin, ney, tin whistle, and the Northumbrian bagpipes could be more audible above the mix. Indeed considerable arrangement of the two bagpipes and the ney – instruments that give the record much of its character – occurred in the studio overdubbing phase.

In the mixing phase, we used considerable amounts of distortion, especially on the bass. As Zagorski-Thomas (2014) has pointed out, techniques like distortion alter, enhance, and 'perhaps even change the meaning of a performance' (82). The decision to use distortion in our case was due to a number of factors – it emerged as a way to put our own sonic mark on traditional music. Fuzz and distortion, especially in the bottom end of the mix, also tend to saturate a recording, having the effect of melding individual parts together, which was an attractive idea given the disparate sounds. It was also an aesthetic choice, based on other recordings that some in the band admired and to some degree emulated, such as *Aeroplanes Over the Sea* by Neutral Milk Hotel (1998; and see Cooper 2005). Distortion generated 'associative meanings' for members of the band with 'particular forms of cultural experience' (Zagorski-Thomas 2014: 86–87). For other members of the band it was novel and unusual. All in all, the combination of the overdubs and the distortion produced a dense, saturated sound, unlike the lighter, more spacious sound of *Northam Avenue*.

Elliot also used Melodyne in key places.[23] This helped to bring some fairly extreme dissonance and inconsistent pitch into line, especially on the bagpipes. The final result is still fairly raw, rough, and ragged, and in fact using Melodyne helped us to find a middle ground – preserving the wildness of the group's aesthetic, yet still being comparable to other pop music recordings. Melodyne represented a compromise that enabled us to bring together vernacular instruments from different cultures, with inconsistent pitch systems, while still making a commercially viable rock record. Like distortion, Melodyne was a kind of glue that held together the various cross-cultural elements.

Audiences (Toby and MohammadReza)

Due to Covid-19 and the fact that Toby moved back to Australia, this project has had limited live public performances. We performed in Huddersfield and York in 2019, and for the Onwards Festival in Huddersfield in 2022. Toby has also performed the songs in Australia, solo or with other musicians who have learnt the parts The audiences for these performances have been largely English-speaking with a pre-existing knowledge and interest in folk and rock.

> Our performances represented cultural diversity and has given the audience the opportunity to experience a different way of performing pop music and the kind of instruments they did not know much about before.

MohammadReza talks about the fact that most of our audiences were hearing the Persian instruments for the first time, and the flow-on effects that had for its reception.

> I realised that for the foreign audience, unlike the Iranian audience, due to the lack of detailed familiarity with the instruments I played and the impossibility of comparison, the quality and output of the work and an attractive performance are more important than technical ability. They evaluated my playing in the format and framework of a pop band, and if I could work within that context I would enhance the quality of the group's work, and consequently would be liked and accepted by the audience. It was obvious that they were excited about getting familiar with new instruments from the Middle East or Iran and having the opportunity to listen to new music. So, while I am introducing these instruments, I am also helping to improve the overall quality of the works.
>
> An Iranian listener's connection with this music is different from that of a stranger. A foreign listener, a European listener, for example, is not familiar with this music. They don't even have a proper understanding of the lyrics to help them imagine this music. Memories associated with a musical genre, which usually make the music familiar to a listener, do not exist for a foreign listener. So, they must make a connection only with the piece of music they

---

[23] A pitch-shifting technology, like autotune but with more nuanced possibilities.

hear and start an imaginary journey to the East based only on the pre-knowledge they already have about the origin of the music.

MohammedReza also talks about the importance of contextualising new instruments for an unfamiliar audience through stage banter.

> Toby's definition of my role in the work is also important in creating a better relationship with the audience. With his presentation and his good relations with the audience, he made the audience expect a new phenomenon in advance.

All this has interesting ramifications vis-à-vis bell hooks' criticisms of the ways in which non-dominant cultures can form a type of 'spice', or Robinson's idea of 'fit'. Inevitably some audiences will find certain instruments and certain performers a novelty. The audiences at an English pop music festival found the neyanban strange and wonderful, while audiences at the Vietnamese Buddhist Tết festival found the sight and sound of an English-speaking Western man singing in Vietnamese different and noteworthy. This is surely one of the delights of music – to present the strange and unexpected in new ways. To bring into being something that seems it should not exist, that does not seem like it belongs (Fisher 2017). This can in fact be a gateway for audiences to engage more fulsomely with unfamiliar performances. However, once through the gate the challenge is then to create something that works, musically, for its own sake. And sometimes it is important to place things in their cultural and regional context so musical elements are grounded and not just floating strange sounds.

The record was released globally in 2021 via Ivy League/Mushroom and received radio play in Australian and British media, in particular 'German Sea' was picked up and added to ABC's Double J. The sense of cultural blending was picked up in reviews of the record, with critics making particular reference to the unusual (in a pop context) instrumentation. Junkee wrote that the record combined 'a myriad of stories', 'traditional folk music', 'peculiar instrumentation and unusual song structures' (Young 2021). Backseat Mafia described the record as 'pastoral pop meets world music' (Kendall 2021). 'Dark Red Blood' is described as beginning with 'weird rhythms and instrumentation: mesmerising and yet at the time faintly disturbing and discomforting, before lilting into a reflective folk-infused and rambling tale' (Kendall 2021). While Town Gossip 'features the Middle Eastern sounds of a flute (ney), creating a lovely tension between a traditional, jangling indie pop song with sweeping strings and something more exotic and mysterious' (Kendall 2021).

As these quotes suggest, Western reviewers tended to note the combining of elements, namely storytelling, British Isles folk music, and Persian sounds. It was also fairly common to describe the rock/folk elements as familiar, with the Persian instrumentation as exotic. This can be ascribed to the fact that most reviewers knew my existing work with folk and rock and thus were comparing it with that, and that they were unfamiliar with the Persian elements.

I Felt the Valley Lifting attempted to do something novel with vernacular forms of folk music. It provided a place where British Isles folk music, southern Iranian folk music, and a punk/garage aesthetic could sit alongside each other in a musically coherent way. This was dependent to a large degree on the flexibility of the musicians, particularly the ability of MohammadReza to recontexualise his performance styles. This, in turn, was dependent on his experience playing Bushehri folk music, which itself was composed of many multicultural ingredients (as outlined in Section 5). It also demonstrated that such coherence was partially dependent on building a level of trust and friendship before the project started and working on projects together outside the central project.

9 Conclusions

In keeping with our two research aims outlined in the introduction, we have several points to make in conclusion that are both pragmatic and theoretical/ conceptual.

Time

Time is important. It is the key that makes all the other points possible. All three projects discussed here were undertaken over an extended period: *Songs from Northam Avenue* took four years; *Song Khúc Lượn Bay/ Two Sounds Gliding* has taken five years and is still ongoing; *I Felt the Valley Lifting* took a year, but was informed by collaborations a year before that. Time helped enable all the players to develop a musical language that worked with each others' and to develop more equitable relationships. The fact that time is so important is not a convenient conclusion. Not everyone has the time, nor the budget, to allow long projects – however, if time can be found, we think it is important. Time is also important for getting to know one's collaborators and building trust. While Lan thought that connection and trust were established from the outset through the collaborators having known each other in previous lives and having compatible zodiacs, MohammadReza and Toby thought that friendship and trust were achieved over time and that trust enabled productive music making. Whatever the angle, all three of us thought that the social connection of music making was important, trust needed to be established first, and time was important, whether the time scale was a few years, or a few thousand years.

Power and Love

Power imbalances cannot be negated, but they can be mindfully dealt with. We found that hooks' idea of a love ethic was a productive way to negotiate the power imbalances inherent in our projects, as were ideas of artistic citizenship. The idea of loving 'across' difference was a fruitful way to think about collaborations and resonated with Buddhist ideas of the negation of the self. Conversely, ideas of love also revolved around the idea of respecting difference. Each collaborator brought something different to the projects, and that difference needed to be respected. There are many examples of the ways in which both connecting across difference, and respecting difference, played out in these projects: from the technical/musical ideas of blending sounds, or placing certain sounds, or even melodic sections such as the Persian Hajiuni, alongside others; to the bigger cultural ideas of using different methods of composition and recording, and sharing elements of our cultures with each other. Each project did this to different degrees. *Two Sounds Gliding* was the deepest negotiation of these things, as it was initiated equally, had more democratic decision making and, consequently, a more democratic structure with associated arguments and negotiations (which was made possible by Lan and Toby's long-term musical relationship and friendship and previous experience working together on *Songs from Northam Avenue*).

Non-musical Things

Part of the importance of time was the importance of doing non-musical things together. When any of the three of us speak or write about the experience of making music together, it doesn't take long for us to start talking about the meals we have shared together, whether one-on-one, with other friends or bandmates, or with our families. Gathering around the table before or after projects, or for particular celebrations, has an important effect on developing connection and allowing us to discuss things that are not about music, but nevertheless feed into our music making.

It is not just meals, it is also doing things that are not directly related to the projects. MohammadReza and Toby facilitated songwriting workshops for refugees in Huddersfield and have taught students at the University of Huddersfield together. Toby was Lan's student in her tai chi and kung fu classes and Lan has been to the University of Sydney to talk to and teach Toby's students. In doing these activities we travel together, talk on the phone, discuss things over tea. Such sharing has an inestimable impact on the projects. It is an obvious point perhaps but one we all feel is vital. Further, cross-cultural projects should be responsive to individual needs, namely work and families, as musicians from different backgrounds can have very different life pressures.

Unfixing/Unsticking

We think it is important to be open to surprises when working on music together. This is, once again, related to time, as sometimes it takes time to get past preconceptions and produce opportunities for surprising things to happen. This works both for the ways we think about ourselves and the ways we think about others. We found that it was important not to 'fix' one's collaborators and the music they play. Toby originally approached Lan because he was looking for a đàn bầu and đàn tranh player, but had no idea, for instance, that she was a singer and that they would end up writing and singing songs together. And, for that matter, that she would translate, arrange, and sing a poem by Lord Byron from the Western literature canon. And why not? Just as Western musicians enjoy exploring other cultures, often through translation, non-Western musicians have that right too.

Conversely, it is important not to 'fix' ourselves, but rather to look for experiences that are transformative and act against fear. Toby had no idea he would sing in Vietnamese, and indeed thought it culturally inappropriate to do so. Yet for Lan, teaching a Vietnamese song brought her a large amount of pleasure, and novelty, and she was very keen to work on this side of the project. It ended up being an important way to share musical culture. MohammadReza also talks about how these projects were a learning experience, an opportunity to take something away.

> This was an opportunity to experience a different cultural approach in the field of music making. For me, having a research perspective and constantly learning, all the moments working with this group were valuable because I was confronted with a culture that had a different flavour than what I had ever dealt with.

Aural Process

This Element is, in large part, an argument for making music by ear. We jammed, listened, improvised, came up with parts by ear, recorded those parts on our phones, listened back, jammed again, changed parts. We found that this process allowed each musician to bring their own performance to the project, rather than being limited to what the composer, or songwriter, had fixed into text. All three of us have had a musical education that has elements of 'reading' music as well as playing by ear. But it is the aural process that we worked with. MohammadReza was educated through the folk music of Bushehr, providing un-notated music for celebrations and concerts; Lan plays a repertoire of Vietnamese music and styles that she knows intimately by ear; I primarily communicated my ideas with bands verbally and through the music itself. Much of the literature on cross-cultural collaboration assumes an art music perspective of a single composer communicating with a group of musicians from various cultural backgrounds via notation. We think it is important to say that there are other models that might work quite well.

Recontextualisation

All the projects discussed here involved making changes to existing ways of doing things and playing things. This process extended from the detailed and technical, such as using different tunings, different strings, different chanters, and using instruments as harmonic accompaniment rather than melodic lead, to the more conceptual, such as adapting and recontextualising performance practices and letting them sit within new scenarios, or in new houses to extend MohammadReza's earlier metaphor. The examples are many: from changing the tuning on Toby's guitar, to Lan getting different strings for her đàn bầu; from a traditional Vietnamese song like 'Wind on the Bridge' played with a rock backing and given a new 'Western' or 'Australian' sound, to Persian and Arabic modes being set within a folk-rock song. Recontextualisation was often the key that allowed the musicians to stay true to a culturally grounded and authentic performance practice, while still creating a 'new way'. In some examples, this process meant that different performances were amalgamated together to create something new or were allowed to sit alongside each other as points of difference. We think that both ways can be representative of a shared democratic method, and both can produce rich musical outcomes.

Money and Control

None of these projects provided anyone with a huge income (although they were important as 'research outputs' and subsequent career advantage for MohammadReza and Toby, as is this Element, and as such have had an indirect financial benefit). The sense of power and control came as much from how the projects were initiated and commissioned as from how the money was distributed. For *Songs from Northam Avenue* and *I Felt the Valley Lifting* I directly employed musicians after the songs were written. I received a lump sum from the University of Huddersfield, calculated costs, and distributed the remaining money equally amongst all the players. These were not high-paying gigs for any of us, and we have had more remunerative performance opportunities. Rather than financial gain, it was pleasure in working with the ensemble, experience playing with different musicians, creative expression, career advancement, artistic citizenship, sociability, and camaraderie. All the things that make music making enjoyable when the money is not there. However, it was the fact that the projects were established before all musicians came on board and Toby was facilitating and directly paying everyone that affected the depth of collaboration.

Two Sounds Gliding, or *Songs from Home* as it was originally named, was differently organised. Lan and Toby were both commissioned by Urban Theatre Projects, and paid the same fee for the original week's development. We subsequently worked on the songs in our own time, unpaid by an external source, except for the performance fee we received from Casula Powerhouse (which once again was split equally and with the other musicians). Concerts were sometimes organised by Lan, and sometimes by Toby. This arrangement was an important contributing factor in the equality of this project. Consequently, Toby has also done things outside his comfort zone, such as singing in Vietnamese, indicating someone else is also in control. Once again, this is evidence of a movement away from fear to love via an equitable and trusting relationship. For the recordings, Bob Scott's engineering fee was paid by the University of Sydney, while Lan paid Phi Le's engineering fee. This did mean that the recordings themselves had somewhat unequal feelings of control – with Toby being more directing in the Scott recordings, and Lan in the Li recordings. All in all, it is fair to conclude that how projects are managed, commissioned, and budgeted affects the working relationship of the musicians. This is always the case, but especially so in a cross-cultural context. The more involved musicians are in the initiation of the projects, the deeper the cross-cultural connections.

Insights into Non-musical Things

In Section 3 of this Element we discussed the ways in which practice-based research in popular music can develop insights about non-musical things, such as social issues. This is not the main focus of this investigation, yet there are a couple of things to note here. Firstly, making music cross-culturally using a pop process provides some insights into how we might develop personal connections across cultures. Listening to each other, learning alongside each other, becoming involved in each other's lives and families, sharing meals together – these are all key parts of making music together but can also be transferred to everyday life and can be thought of metaphorically in non-musical life. Secondly, the broad appeal of these projects and their musical coherence indicates that musical cultures are not so different to each other as we might think. Given enough time and the right strategies, musical styles that are not supposed to go together find an audience together. This has implications for stereotypes more broadly that assume that migrant cultures ghettoise and can't assimilate. We show here ways in which different cultures and people can merge sounds and approaches, yet still retain a cultural distinctiveness.

Generation of Knowledge through a Pop Music Practice

We have placed our work within a context of practice-based research in other types of arts practices and academic disciplines. Knowledge from these other practices and disciplines has informed our work; however, we also think that that the particular strategies of popular music have something to add to practice-based research generally. These strategies include prioritising collaborative practice, and taking an organic, slow-paced approach to the dynamics of this collaboration (as bands tend to do); experimenting with the line between autobiography and fiction in songwriting; and thinking about how very specific, and often not frequently heard, voices and experiences may develop a more general, even universal appeal. A pop process might not just produce catchy songs, but also new knowledge.

References

Adlington R and Buch E (2020) Introduction: Looking for Democracy in Music and Elsewhere. In Adlington R and Buch E (eds.), *Finding Democracy in Music*. London: Routledge, 1–18.

Ahmad MM (2013) Western Sydney Deserves to Be Written About, *The Guardian*. July 18.

Ahmed S (2012) *On Being Included: Racism and Diversity in Institutional Life*. Durham, NC: Duke University Press.

Baily J (2001) Learning to Perform as a Research Technique in Ethnomusicology. *British Journal of Ethnomusicology* 10(2), 85–98.

Barney K and Proud M (2014) Collaborative Music Research at the Contact Zone in Cherbourg, and Aboriginal Community in Queensland. In Barney K (ed.), *Collaborative Ethnomusicology: New Approaches to Music Research between Indigenous and Non-Indigenous Australians*. Melbourne: Lyrebird Press, 81–96.

Bartleet BL (2016) The Role of Love in Intercultural Arts Theory and Practice. In Burnard P, Mackinlay E, and Powell K (eds.), *The Routledge International Handbook on Intercultural Arts Research*. London: Routledge, 91–101.

Bartleet BL and Carfoot G (2016) Arts-Based Service Learning with Indigenous Communities: Engendering Artistic Citizenship. Chapter 17 in Elliott DJ, Silverman M, and Bowman WD (eds.), *Artistic Citizenship: Artistry, Social Responsibility, and Ethical Praxis*. New York, NY: Oxford University Press. DOI: https://doi.org/10.1093/acprof:oso/9780199393749.001.0001.

Beladi SM (2021) *Music of Bushehr and Its Origin in the Path of History and Cultural Interactions in Persia*. Tehran: Arvan.

Beladi, SM. (2023). Neyanban and its Role in the Music of Bushehr [Doctoral thesis]. Huddersfield: University of Huddersfield. Retrieved from https://pure.hud.ac.uk/en/studentTheses/neyanban-and-its-role-in-the-music-of-bushehr

Blair T (2014) Last Drinks in Lakemba: Tim Blair Takes a Look inside Sydney's Muslim Land. *Daily Telegraph*, 17 August.

Bohlman P (2002) *World Music*. Oxford: Oxford University Press.

Bowman WD (2016) Artistry, Ethics and Citizenship. Chapter 4 in Elliott DJ, Silverman M, and Bowman WD (eds.), *Artistic Citizenship: Artistry, Social Responsibility, and Ethical Praxis*. New York, NY: Oxford University Press. DOI: https://doi.org/10.1093/acprof:oso/9780199393749.001.0001.

Brown M, Pahl K, Rasool Z, and Ward P (2020) Co-producing Research with Communities: Emotions in Community Research. *Global Discourse* 10(2), 93–114.

Campbell G and Puruntatameri TK (2014) When Performance Comes before Research: Reflecting on a Tiwi/Non-Tiwi Musical and Research Collaboration.

In Barney K (ed.), *Collaborative Ethnomusicology: New Approaches to Music Research between Indigenous and Non-Indigenous Australians*. Melbourne: Lyrebird Press, 129–146.

Cantle T (2012) *Interculturalism: For the Era of Cohesion and Diversity*. Basingstoke: Palgrave Macmillan.

Carfoot G (2016) Enough Is Enough: Songs and Messages about Alcohol in Remote Central Australia. *Popular Music* 35(2), 222–230.

Cherry N (2022) The Violin's Bridge between Past and Future (The Fiddler on the Palace Roof): Alfred Hook Lecture. University of Sydney, 25 November. www.youtube.com/watch?v=DA-9T65iMfU.

Clark MK (2021) Hip-Hop and Pan-Africanism: From Blitz the Ambassador to Beyoncé, *The Conversation*, 29 January 2021. https://theconversation.com/hip-hop-and-pan-africanism-from-blitz-the-ambassador-to-beyonce-151680, accessed 10 January 2023.

Collinson-Scott J (2018) Pop as Research. https://popasresearch.com/, accessed 16 November 2018.

Cooper K (2005) *In the Aeroplane Over the Sea*. 33 1/3 Continuum Publishing. New York, NY: Bloomsbury.

Dawe K (2015) The Many Worlds of Popular Music: Ethnomusicological Approaches. In Bennett A and Waksman S (eds.), *The Sage Handbook of Popular Music*. Thousand Oaks, CA: Sage, 15–32.

Edwards I, Hammond N, and Sollberger E (eds.) (1975) *The Cambridge Ancient History, History of the Middle East and the Aegean Region c. 1380–1000 B.C.* (3rd ed., Vol. 2, Part 2). New York, NY: Cambridge University Press.

Elkins J (2005) The Three Configurations of Practice-Based PhDs. *Printed Project* 4, 7–19.

Elliott DJ, Silverman M, and Bowman WD (2016) Artistic Citizenship: Introduction, Aims and Overview. Chapter 1 in Elliott DJ, Silverman M, and Bowman WD (eds.), *Artistic Citizenship: Artistry, Social Responsibility, and Ethical Praxis*. New York, NY: Oxford University Press. DOI: https://doi.org/10.1093/acprof:oso/9780199393749.001.0001.

Erlmann V (1999) *Music, Modernity and the Global Imagination. South Africa and the West*. New York: Oxford University Press.

Exarchos M (aka Stereo Mike) (2020) Sonic Necessity and Compositional Invention in #BluesHop. *Journal of Popular Music Studies* 32(3), 99–119.

Fabian J (1983) *Time and the Other: How Anthropology Makes Its Object*. New York, NY: Columbia University Press.

Farraj J and Shumays SB (2019) *Arabic Maqam Performance and Theory in the 20th Century*. Oxford: Oxford University Press.

Fisher M (2017) *The Weird and the Eerie*. London: Repeater Books.

Frith S (1996) Music and Identity. In Hall S and du Gay P (eds.), *Questions of Cultural Identity*, London: Sage, 108–127.

Gilroy P (2002) *There Ain't No Black in the Union Jack*. London: Routledge.

Hage G (1998) *White Nation: Fantasies of White Supremacy in a Multicultural Society*. Melbourne: Pluto Press.

Harper P, Aruz J, and Tallon F (1992) *The Royal City of Susa: Ancient Near Eastern Treasures in the Louvre*. New York, NY: Metropolitan Museum of Art.

Hitchins R (2013) Rhythm, Sound and Movement: The Guitarist as Participant-Observer in Jamaica's Studio Culture. In Dawe K (ed.), *Guitar Ethnographies: Performance, Technology and Material Culture.* Special issue of *Ethnomusicology Forum*, 22(1), 27–48.

Hood M (1982) *The Ethnomusicologist*. Kent, OH: Kent State University Press.

hooks b (1992) Eating the Other: Desire and Resistance. Chapter 3 in hooks b, *Black Looks: Race and Representation*. Boston, MA: South End Press.

hooks b (2000) *All About Love: New Visions*. New York, NY: William Morrow.

hooks b (2014) *Ain't I A Woman*, 2nd edition. Abingdon: Routledge.

hooks b and Hall S (2017) *Uncut Funk: A Contemplative Dialogue*. London: Taylor and Francis.

hooks b and Yancy G (2015) bell hooks: Buddhism, the Beats and Loving Blackness. *New York Times*, 10 December. https://archive.nytimes.com/opi nionator.blogs.nytimes.com/2015/12/10/bell-hooks-buddhism-the-beats-and-loving-blackness/, accessed 11 October 2023.

Hughes S, Pennington JL, and Makris S (2012) Translating Autoethnography across the AERA Standards: Toward Understanding Autoethnographic Scholarship as Empirical Research. *Educational Researcher* 41(6), 209–219.

Huxtable P (2014) *Sound System Culture: Celebrating Huddersfield's Sound Systems*, One Love Books.

Ingold T (2013) *Making: Anthropology, Art and Architecture*. Abdingdon: Routledge.

Kendall A (2021) Album Review: Youth Group's Toby Martin's Solo Album 'I Felt The Valley Lifting'. *Backseat Mafia*, 9 November. www.backseatmafia .com/album-review-youth-groups-toby-martins-solo-album-i-felt-the-val ley-lifting-is-an-uplifting-amalgam-of-mystical-realism-and-the-minutiae-of-everyday-life/, accessed 3 February 2023.

Koszolko MK (2017) The Giver: A Case Study of the Impact of Remote Music Collaboration Software on Music Production Process. *IASPM Journal*. Special issue: *Practice-Led and Practice-Based Popular Music Studies* 7(2), 32–40.

Lacasse S and Stévance S (2017) *Research-Creation in Music and the Arts: Towards a Collaborative Interdiscipline*. London: Taylor and Francis.

Laughter J (2014) Toward a Theory of Micro-kindness: Developing Positive Actions in Multicultural Education. *International Journal of Multicultural Education* 16(2), 2–14.

Lorde A (2007a) The Uses of the Erotic: The Erotic as Power. In Lorde A, *Sister Outsider*. New York: Penguin, 53–59.

Lorde A (2007b) Age, Race, Class, and Sex: Women Redefining Difference. In Lorde A, *Sister Outsider*. New York: Penguin, 114–123.

Macdonald A (2021) I Felt the Valley Lifting (Album Documentary). https://www.youtube.com/watch?v=7w_OweWgenE&t=346s, accessed 8 March 2023.

Mackinlay E and Chalmers G (2014) Remembrances and Relationships: Rethinking Collaborative Ethnomusicology as Ethical and Decolonising Practice. In Barney K (ed.), *Collaborative Ethnomusicology: New Approaches to Music Research between Indigenous and Non-Indigenous Australians*. Melbourne: Lyrebird Press, 63–80.

Manning E (2016) *The Minor Gesture*. Durham, NC: Duke University Press.

Markus A (1994) *Australian Race Relations*. Sydney: Allen and Unwin.

Marsh K (2012) 'The Beat Will Make You Be Courage': The Role of a Secondary School Music Program in Supporting Young Refugees and Newly Arrived Immigrants in Australia. *Research Studies in Music Education* 34(2), 93–111.

McKerrell S (2022) Towards Practice Research in Ethnomusicology. *Ethnomusicology Forum* 31(1), 10–27.

McLaughlin S (2015) Scott Mc Laughlin Reporting on a PaR Discussion. *Artistic Research Reports* [blog]. http://artisticresearchreports.blogspot.com.au/2015/12/scott-mc-laughlin-reporting-on-par.html?spref=fb, accessed 1 April 2018.

Mera M (2015) Can Composition and Performance Be Research? Talk given at City University, 25 November. https://blogs.city.ac.uk/music/tag/composition-as-research/, accessed 1 April 2018.

Meredith J (2017) *Songs from Northam Avenue: Mini Documentary*. https://vimeo.com/195744782, accessed 7 August 2024.

Nærland TU (2014) Rhythm, Rhyme and Reason: Hip Hop Expressivity as Political Discourse. *Popular Music* 33, 473–491.

Nelson R (2013) *Practice-Based Research in the Arts: Principles, Protocols, Pedagogies, Resistances*. London: Palgrave Macmillan.

Nettl B (1995) *Heartland Excursions*. Urbana, IL: University of Illinois Press.

Neutral Milk Hotel (1998) *In the Aeroplane Over the Sea*. Chapel Hill, NC: Merge Records.

Nooshin L (2014) Introduction. In Nooshin L (ed.), *The Ethnomusicology of Western Art Music*. London: Routledge, 1–16.

Norton B (2009) *Songs for the Spirits: Music and Mediums in Modern Vietnam.* Urbana, IL: University of Illinois Press.

Östersjö S, Thủy NT, Hebert DG, and Frisk H (2023) *Shared Listenings: Methods for Transcultural Musicianship and Research.* Cambridge: Cambridge University Press.

Pham S (2022) Western Sydney Is Dead, Long Live Western Sydney! *Sydney Review of Books*, 14 June. https://sydneyreviewofbooks.com/essay/western-sydney-is-dead-long-live-western-sydney/, accessed 13 March 2023.

Read P (2000) *Belonging: Australians, Place and Aboriginal Ownership.* Cambridge: Cambridge University Press.

Robinson D (2020) *Hungry Listening: Resonant Theory for Indigenous Sound Studies.* Minneapolis, MN: University of Minnesota Press.

Rodano R and Olanyian T (2016) *Audible Empire: Music, Global Politics, Critique.* Durham, NC: Duke University Press.

Ross V (2016) Framing Intercultural Music Composition Research. In Burnard P, Mackinlay E, and Powell K (eds.), *The Routledge International Handbook on Intercultural Arts Research.* London: Routledge, 431–443.

Sahota HS (2014) *Bhangra: Mystics, Music and Migration.* Huddersfield: University of Huddersfield Press.

SarrouyAD (2023) El Sistema. Athens, Greece. Report.

ShukerR (2016) *Understanding Popular Music.* Fifth edition. London: Routledge.

Smith B (2017) Youth Group's Toby Martin on His New Solo Album and Being an Outsider in Western Sydney. *The Guardian.* 21 February. www.theguardian.com/music/2017/feb/21/youth-groups-toby-martin-on-his-new-solo-album-and-being-an-outsider-in-western-sydney, accessed 7 August 2024.

Smith LT (1999) *Decolonizing Methodologies: Research and Indigenous People.* London: Zed Books.

Somerville M (2014) Creative Collaborations in the Contact Zone. In Barney K (ed.), *Collaborative Ethnomusicology: New Approaches to Music Research between Indigenous and Non-Indigenous Australians.* Melbourne: Lyrebird Press, 9–24.

Summerskill C (2020) *Creating Verbatim Theatre from Oral Histories.* London: Routledge.

Tagg P (2011) Caught on the Back Foot: Epistemic Inertia and Invisible Music. *IASPM Journal* 2, 1–2.

Tâm TT (1991) *Buddhism of Wisdom and Faith: Pure Land Principles and Practice.* Sepulvada, CA: International Buddhist Monastic Institute.

Torgovnik M (1990) *Gone Primitive: Savage Intellects, Modern Lives.* Chicago, IL: University of Chicago Press.

Turino T (2003). Are We Global Yet? Globalist Discourse, Cultural Formations and the Study of Zimbawbean Popular Music, *British Journal of Ethnomusicology* 12(2), 51–79.

Turino T (2016) Music, Social Change, and Alternative Forms of Citizenship. In Elliott DJ, Silverman M, and Bowman WD (eds.), *Artistic Citizenship: Artistry, Social Responsibility, and Ethical Praxis*. New York, NY: Oxford University Press, 297–312.

Urie A, McNeill F, Frödén LC et al. (2019) Reintegration, Hospitality and Hostility: Song-writing and Song-Sharing in Criminal Justice. *Journal of Extreme Anthropology* 3(1), 77–110.

van de Merwe P (1992) *Origins of the Popular Style: The Antecedents of Twentieth Century Popular Music*. Oxford: Oxford University Press.

Various artists (2018) *Not Known at This Address*. Glasgow: Vox Liminis.

Vougioukalou S, Dow R, Bradshaw L, and Pallant T (2019) Wellbeing and Integration through Community Music: The Role of Improvisation in a Music Group of Refugees, Asylum Seekers and Local Community Members. *Contemporary Music Review* 38(5), 533–548.

Wolinski P (2017) Fully Automated Luxury Composition. *IASPM Journal*. Special Issue: Practice-Led and Practice-Based Popular Music Studies 7(2), 8–15.

Young DJ (2017) Toby Martin: Songs from Northam Avenue Review. *Rolling Stone*, February.

Young DJ (2021) 20 Incredible Australian Albums That Flew under the Radar This Year. *Junkee*, 14 December. https://junkee.com/australian-albums-underrated-2021/317847, accessed 3 February 2023.

Zagorski-Thomas S (2014) *The Musicology of Record Production*. Cambridge: Cambridge University Press.

Acknowledgements

Much of the research and music-making that grounds this Element took place on Aboriginal land. We acknowledge and pay our respects to Gadigal, Wangal, and Dharug elders past, present and emerging. Other parts of this Element were researched and written in north-west England, which financially benefited from and was essentially built on the production of wool and cotton during the Industrial Revolution: materials that came directly from the colonial seizure of Indigenous lands.

We would like to thank the other wonderful musicians who were involved in the projects discussed here: Bree van Reyk, Mohammed Lelo, Alex Hadchiti, Maroun Azar, Cameron Emerson-Elliott, Matthew Steffen, Zoe Hauptmann, Phong Phu, Anh Linh Pham, Chris Ruffoni, George Harrington, Sarah Tym, and Julia Morgan. Our sincere thanks to them for their talents and their contribution to making new music and creating new knowledge. The engineers on these projects – Bob Scott and Colin Elliot – were also instrumental in shepherding and capturing our often unruly sound Lyndal Irons' photos and videos have provided important and beautiful visual context for *Songs from Northam Avenue* and Two Sounds Gliding, as did Cameron Emerson-Elliott's design for *I Felt the Valley Lifting*.

Thank you to Urban Theatre Projects (Utp), and in particular their then Artistic Director Rosie Dennis, whose support for two of these projects at inception was critical. Thank you Rosie for commissioning, supporting and staging these works and for the conversations over felafel and mint tea. Gratitude too to David and Catherine Cranston for hosting Toby in the first songwriting residency and providing the first venue for the *Songs from Northam Avenue* performance, and to Michael for hosting too. Thanks as well to the other institutions who have released music and staged concerts: Ivy League Records, Onwards Festival (and Sam Hodgson), Casula Powerhouse, Carriageworks (and Lisa French), and Sydney Festival.

These projects were funded by research grants from the University of Huddersfield and the University of Sydney and we would like to acknowledge the support and collegiality offered by our colleagues there.

Thank you to the commissioning editor of the 21st Century Music Practice series, Simon Zagorski-Thomas, for his interest in this research and his support, and to the publishing team at Cambridge University Press, especially Kate Brett.

Thank you to members of the University of Sydney Conservatorium of Music, WIP (Work in Progress) group for giving valuable feedback on an early draft – Amanda Harris, Chris Coady, Jadey O'Regan, Catherine Ingram, and Georgia Curran – and to the anonymous reviewers of this Element.

Toby has also also appreciated the opportunity to talk through ideas with Jo Collinson-Scott, and to read and hear her work, which inspired ours.

Thanks to our students for trying for testing out some these ideas in classes.

And thanks to our families – Jane, Ada, Eugene, Shery, Ali, Daniel, and Pham – for their love.

Cambridge Elements ≡

Twenty-First Century Music Practice

Simon Zagorski-Thomas

London College of Music, University of West London

Simon Zagorski-Thomas is a Professor at the London College of Music (University of West London, UK) and founded and runs the 21st Century Music Practice Research Network. He is series editor for the Cambridge Elements series and Bloomsbury book series on 21st Century Music Practice. He is ex-chairman and co-founder of the Association for the Study of the Art of Record Production. He is a composer, sound engineer and producer and is, currently, writing a monograph on practical musicology. His books include *Musicology of Record Production* (2014; winner of the 2015 IASPM Book Prize), *The Art of Record Production: an Introductory Reader for a New Academic Field* co-edited with Simon Frith (2012), the *Bloomsbury Handbook of Music Production* co-edited with Andrew Bourbon (2020) and the *Art of Record Production: Creative Practice in the Studio* co-edited with Katia Isakoff, Serge Lacasse and Sophie Stévance (2020).

About the Series

Elements in Twenty-First Century Music Practice has developed out of the 21st Century Music Practice Research Network, which currently has around 250 members in 30 countries and is dedicated to the study of what Christopher Small termed musicking – the process of making and sharing music rather than the output itself. Obviously this exists at the intersection of ethnomusicology, performance studies, and practice pedagogy / practice-led-research in composition, performance, recording, production, musical theatre, music for screen and other forms of multi-media musicking. The generic nature of the term '21st Century Music Practice' reflects the aim of the series to bring together all forms of music into a larger discussion of current practice and to provide a platform for research about any musical tradition or style. It embraces everything from hip-hop to historically informed performance and K-pop to Inuk throat singing.

Cambridge Elements ☰

Twenty-First Century Music Practice

Printed in the United States
by Baker & Taylor Publisher Services